Good Places to Live

Poverty and Public Housing in Canada

Jim Silver

Fernwood Publishing • Halifax & Winnipeg

To Loa Henry
for her constant love and support

Editing: Brenda Conroy
Cover Artwork: Unknown artist, participant in December 2008
Little Mountain, Citywide Housing Coalition artists and activists event
Cover Photo: Matthew Rogers
Cover Design: John van der Woude
Printed and bound in Canada by Hignell Book Printing

Published in Canada by Fernwood Publishing
32 Oceanvista Lane
Black Point, Nova Scotia, B0J 1B0
and 748 Broadway Avenue, Winnipeg, Manitoba, R3G 0X3
www.fernwoodpublishing.ca

Fernwood Publishing Company Limited gratefully acknowledges the financial support of the
Government of Canada through the Canada Book Fund, the Canada Council for the Arts, the
Nova Scotia Department of Tourism and Culture and the Province of Manitoba, through the
Book Publishing Tax Credit, for our publishing program.

Library and Archives Canada Cataloguing in Publication

Silver, Jim, 1946-
Good places to live : poverty and public housing in Canada / Jim
Silver.

Includes bibliographical references.
ISBN 978-1-55266-414-8

1. Public housing--Canada. 2. Urban poor--Housing--Canada.
I. Title.

HD7288.78.C3S55 2011   363.585'0971   C2010-908029-7

Contents

Acknowledgements

A great many people have been good enough to help me with this project in a wide variety of ways over the past four years. I am happy to have the opportunity to acknowledge all of them, and I apologize to anyone I may inadvertently have missed.

In Winnipeg I have been privileged to work, and I look forward to that continuing, at Lord Selkirk Park in the heart of the North End with many wonderful people. I am happy to acknowledge the support of the following, who have been involved with various aspects of the work at Lord Selkirk Park and the North End Community Renewal Corporation: Dianne Barron, Candi Beardy, Mearle Chief, Gary Comack, Jeff Deitz, Betty Edel, Christa Furst, Cheyenne Henry, Nanette McKay, Rob Neufeld, Duchant Persaud, Greg Slobodeski, Brenda Wild and the late Tom Yauk. I particularly acknowledge my friends Janice Goodman of the North End Community Renewal Corporation and Carolyn Young of Manidoo Gi Miini Gonaan, with whom I have worked especially closely in recent years, as well as all of those, including adult education students and residents, associated with the Lord Selkirk Park Resource Centre, Kaakiyow Li Moond Likol, the Tots and Families program and the Community Advisory Committee. Provincial cabinet ministers Kerri Irvin-Ross, Diane McGifford and Gord McIntosh have been very supportive, as have my friends and colleagues at the Canadian Centre for Policy Alternatives-Manitoba and our Manitoba Research Alliance on Transforming Inner-City and Aboriginal Communities, especially Errol Black, Lynne Fernandez, John Loxley and Shauna MacKinnon. The following people have provided research assistance in one form or another in Winnipeg: Elizabeth Bingus, David Burley, Joy Goertzen, Matt Hamilton, Pam Hotomani, Claudette Michell, Laura Reimer, Jennifer Seaton, Maya Seshia and Jake Wark. I am particularly indebted to Matt Rogers, who worked with me on all four of the public housing projects, both while completing an undergraduate degree at the University of Winnipeg and while doing a graduate degree at the University of British Columbia, and who did a superb job in everything that he took on. Thank you Matt.

In Halifax I am happy to acknowledge the support and contributions of the following people who live and/or work in and around Uniacke Square, all of whom were unfailingly generous with their time and their ideas: Irvine Carvery, John Fleming, Melissa Grant, Darcy Harvey, Claudia Jahn, Gregg

Lambert, Claudie Levy, Maureen MacDonald, Amy MacKay, Joan Mendes, Peter Mortimer, Tyler Morton, Paul O'Hara, Dawn Sloane, Jenise Smith, Wade Smith and Grant Wanzel. I am particularly grateful to Donna Nelligan, long-time resident of Uniacke Square and community worker extraordinaire, and to the residents of Uniacke Square who agreed to be interviewed by Donna.

In Vancouver I am happy to acknowledge the contributions of Cameron Gray, Ben Johnson, Kia Salomans and Ellen Woodsworth, plus the approximately twenty residents and former residents of Little Mountain Housing who agreed to lengthy and informative interviews with Matt Rogers.

In Toronto, where I visited Regent Park numerous times in recent years and where people were extremely generous in meeting and talking with me, I am pleased to acknowledge the contributions of Carolyn Acker, Andrew Allan, Martine August, Derek Ballantyne, Bill Blair, Lucky Boothe, Chris Brillinger, Judy Brooks, Margarite Campbell, Neil Clarke, Karen Cooper, Debra Dineen, Sharmini Fernando, Paula Fletcher, Coreen Gilligan, Catherine Goulet, Brian Holden, Andrea Hylton, Sharon Kelly, David Kidd, Jeff Kugler, Joe Leibovich, Cheryl MacDonald, Diane MacLean, Pam McConnell, Sean Meagher, Phil Nazar, Bethany Osborne, Norman Rowen, John Sewell, Mandy Swinamer and Hugh Wong. I am especially grateful to the more than seventy residents of Regent Park who took the time to speak with me during my last two research trips about their thoughts on the redevelopment of Regent Park, and to Gene Lincoln, long-time community youth worker whose intimate knowledge of Regent Park and the people who live there is remarkable.

I gratefully acknowledge the generous financial support of the Social Sciences and Humanities Research Council of Canada, by way both of a Standard Research Grant and a Community-University Research Alliance (CURA) grant held by the Manitoba Research Alliance on "Transforming Inner-City and Aboriginal Communities" and administered by the Canadian Centre for Policy Alternatives-Manitoba.

Finally, I am pleased to acknowledge the support of all the people at Fernwood Publishing — Beverley Rach, Debbie Mathers, Brenda Conroy, Nancy Malek and John van der Woude — and especially my long-time friend Wayne Antony, for their work on this book and for their ongoing support for my work.

Chapter 1

Good Places to Live

I have been heavily influenced in the writing of this book by my ongoing experience at Lord Selkirk Park (LSP), a 314-unit public housing project in Winnipeg's low-income North End. When I began work there, most community workers offered a bleak assessment of prevailing conditions, and I was originally affected by this negative disposition. However, the more I became involved at LSP, the more positively I have grown to feel about the place and its residents. Working closely with many people in the community, and guided by community development principles (Silver and Loxley 2007) and by the expressed interests and needs of residents of LSP, a small group of community workers has managed to play a positive role in the creation of a number of institutions. Lord Selkirk Park is already in some ways a different place than it was in 2005, and although many problems still remain, it will continue to improve as a place to live as long as we and the residents who live there are able to continue on the path that we are now on.

The case for optimism was made especially clear to me at the June 18, 2010, graduation ceremony for eleven adult learners at Kaakiyow Li Moond Likel (a Michif name meaning All Peoples' School), which is an adult learning centre offering the mature grade twelve diploma, which we started in September 2007. The ceremony took place in Turtle Island Community Centre, in the heart of LSP, where classes are held. A twenty-four-year-old Aboriginal woman, who had graduated the year before and had just completed her first year of post-secondary education at Red River College, spoke to those of us assembled for the celebration. She described dropping out of school in grade ten because of alcohol and drug addiction and related problems, and said that she had come back to Kaakiyow two years ago to give education another try in a more community-like setting. Mearle Chief, one of the two outstanding teachers at Kaakiyow (Christa Fuerst is the other; Candi Beardy is the equally outstanding and absolutely necessary support/ outreach worker), told me after the ceremony that when this young woman first came to Kaakiyow she was completely unable to speak in class, so lacking was she in self-confidence and self-esteem. Yet she spoke at the graduation ceremony with grace and poise and told us all about how Kaakiyow had transformed her life. James Cook, one of the 2010 graduates and a (young) grandfather, wrote in the Kaakiyow yearbook that he used to be shy and "felt useless" following years of "living off cheap jobs and partying every other night," but: "That was 10 years ago/Today I live my life different/Instead of drinking/I love to read/Learning new things everyday/Awesome..../My next goal is to become a Social Worker." A long-time resident of LSP told me following the ceremony that her daughter, who also graduated that day, had been deeply depressed and virtually unable to leave their home before starting at Kaakiyow three years before. Now she is a grade twelve graduate planning a career as a childcare worker, and we hope to hire her — consistent with our local hiring strategy — in the childcare/family resource centre, which is another of our projects (because residents have told us that this is what they need). The centre is scheduled to open in September 2011, creating twenty-four local jobs and increased opportunities for parents to earn their grade twelve.

When the provincial minister for Housing and Community Development visited Lord Selkirk Park and Kaakiyow at our invitation in early February 2010, every student in attendance stood, one after the other and without prompting, to tell her that they had experienced a great many problems associated with poverty and racism and the very damaging effects of colonization, and at times they felt hopeless about their futures, but that Kaakiyow was transforming their lives.

Many lives are being transformed at Lord Selkirk Park Housing Developments; the community too is being transformed. Opportunities, tailored to the particular circumstances of residents of LSP, are being created for people to develop their individual capacities and their community in ways of their and their community's choosing. Many are seizing these opportunities. The mood in the Developments (as LSP is called by those in the North End) is becoming noticeably more positive, and residents are gradually stepping forward to say that they too want to be involved with the many good things going on there.

Poverty and Public Housing

This book is about urban poverty and large, inner-city public housing projects. The two usually go together — but they need not. Public housing projects can be good places to live, the negative image notwithstanding. Poverty is solved not by razing public housing projects, as has been the practice throughout North America during the past two decades, but rather by rebuilding public housing communities from within.

Public housing and its residents are stigmatized and stereotyped in ways that obscure more than they reveal and that feed into a long-standing theme in the study of urban poverty that places the blame for their often-difficult circumstances on public housing residents themselves, identifying their behaviour and their cultural attributes as the primary sources of their poverty. The design of large urban public housing projects has also become a popular part of the explanation for public housing woes. While design is an issue and while public housing projects are home to more than their share of destructive and illegal behaviour, the problems typically associated with inner-city public housing are better explained by a combination of socio-economic and historical factors. These include the hollowing out of inner cities due to post-Second World War suburbanization; the de-industrialization associated with an increasingly globalized economy, which has created a labour market particularly disadvantageous to low-income people; the inability of the private, for-profit housing industry to meet Canada's long-standing need for low-income rental housing; the absence of a national housing strategy; the continued power of racism, and in the case of Aboriginal people, of colonization; and the failure of governments, consistent with the neoliberalism of the past thirty years, to invest in a meaningful anti-poverty strategy, and more generally their failure to invest in initiatives that promote equality, rather than ever-increasing inequality. In some cases, Toronto's Regent Park for example, the neoliberal failure to invest has led to the physical deterioration of valuable public housing. In many cases, neoliberal ideas about the redevelopment of deteriorated downtowns have placed nearby public housing projects at risk because higher-income people want the increasingly valuable land on which the public housing and its low-income residents are located.

Four Public Housing Projects

In this book I examine four inner-city public housing projects: Little Mountain Housing in Vancouver; Regent Park in Toronto; Uniacke Square in Halifax; and Lord Selkirk Park in Winnipeg.

Little Mountain was bulldozed in 2009 and 2010. The residents, who insist that Little Mountain was a wonderful place to live and to raise a family, have been scattered. The beautiful location on which it was built lies vacant, while tens of thousands in Vancouver are in need of good quality, low-income rental housing of the kind that Little Mountain provided. Yet the case of Little Mountain is important because it provides empirical evidence that public housing can be a good place to live.

Regent Park in Toronto is in the midst of a massive, fifteen-year or longer redevelopment that will see each of its 2083 units of subsidized housing bulldozed and the location revamped as a mixed-income community, which will, upon completion, have cost a currently estimated $1 billion. Despite this massive cost, the redevelopment will produce no net gain whatever in the number of subsidized housing units, and in fact there will be a net loss of such units on the Regent Park footprint, at a time when there are long wait lists for subsidized housing in Toronto. The redevelopment will displace many long-term residents who consider Regent Park to be home, who feel a strong sense of community in Regent Park and who want to stay. The area, a twenty-minute walk from the Eaton Centre in downtown Toronto, will look better and will offer an attractive downtown location for those who can afford the new condos, but many low-income people will have been moved out.

Uniacke Square is located in a gradually gentrifying North End neighbourhood located a ten-minute walk from downtown Halifax. It faces the risk that its fate, and that of its low-income residents, will be similar to that of the residents of Little Mountain and Regent Park. The land on which Uniacke Square sits may soon become valuable, and that typically means trouble for low-income residents. Any attempt to privatize the public housing units, an idea frequently floated in recent years, which some consider a solution to the problems associated with Uniacke Square, is likely to face concerted opposition from residents. They say that theirs is a tightly knit community in which everyone knows everyone else and where, despite the stigma and stereotypes, they want to stay.

In Winnipeg's Lord Selkirk Park, a different approach is underway. Sheltered from the threat of the bulldozer and of redevelopment in the interests of higher-income people by its location in Winnipeg's very low-income North End, far from a downtown that has been largely unsuccessful in its revitalization efforts to date, it is in the early stages of the Rebuilding from Within strategy, which holds out significant promise for its low-income residents and may yield insight into anti-poverty efforts elsewhere.

To varying degrees, the four public housing projects examined in this book exhibit all of the characteristics of spatially concentrated racialized poverty. As shown in Table 1-1, labour force participation rates, levels of formal education and median incomes are low in each project, while rates of unemployment, proportions of single-parent families and the incidence of poverty, as measured by incomes below the Statistics Canada Low-Income Cut Offs (LICOs) are high. Census Canada data for 2006 show that in Uniacke Square in Halifax, just under half of the residents are of African-Canadian descent; in Winnipeg's Lord Selkirk Park, about two-thirds of residents are Aboriginal; in Regent Park, some eighty-five different languages are spoken; and in Little Mountain, two-thirds of residents were of African or Asian descent.

These high levels of racialized poverty notwithstanding, the process underway at LSP and the long-term success of Vancouver's Little Mountain Housing are evidence that — contrary to popular opinion and contrary to the stigma and stereotypes that fuel that opinion — inner-city public housing projects can be good places to live. Each of the four cases provides evidence of a strong sense of community. That so many large, inner-city public housing projects have been bulldozed is a function less of the flaws of public housing and more of the desirability of the land to those of higher incomes, plus the

Table 1-1 Selected Indicators, Four Public Housing Projects, 2006

Indicator	Little Mountain	Lord Selkirk Park	Regent Park	Uniacke Square
Single-parent families	46.4%	60.5%	42.8%	64.1%
Less than high school (20+)	32.8%	58.7%	42.8%	24.0%
Adult unemployment rate (25+)	11.6%	18.7%	19.7%	15.3%
Adult labour force participation (25+)	71.7%	39.5%	49.7%	68.6%
Female labour force participation (25+)	74.3%	28.2%	40.4%	64.2%
Youth labour force participation (15–24)	84.2%	37.7%	49.3%	55.5%
Median household income	$37,010	$15,552	$29,511	$28,000
% below LICO	35.7%	82.8%	67.9%	64.0%

Source: Statistics Canada, Census of Canada

willingness of neoliberal governments to displace the poor in the interests of the more well-to-do. This displacement is made the more poignant by the severe shortage across the country of low-income rental housing. The alternative to the bulldozer is the long, slow, grassroots process of community development being undertaken at Lord Selkirk Park.

There are limits to this grassroots approach, but it is the necessary but not sufficient condition for the transformation of public housing in ways of residents' choosing. The limits have to do with the failure of neoliberal governments to use the all-important tool of public investment to the extent that is necessary to solve the complex problems of spatially concentrated racialized poverty. Building on the strengths of low-income public housing projects — the strong sense of community, the good quality of the rental housing in those cases when it has not been deliberately allowed to physically deteriorate, the many strong and healthy individuals and families who live there, for example — is the conceptual and practical starting point. But the process will be stalled at an early stage in the absence of meaningful public investment in those institutions — resource centres, adult education facilities, childcare centres, for example — that residents identify as being what they need to transform their lives and their communities in ways of their choosing. Public investment on the scale that is necessary, however, is directly counter to the ideological temper of the times, which leads governments to disinvest rather than to invest at the lower end of the income scale.

What this book shows is that large, inner-city public housing projects have many more strengths than most people think and that, rather than being torn down in the interests of higher-income people when low-income rental housing is already in short supply, they should and can be rebuilt from within, using an asset-based and resident-driven form of community development supported by meaningful public investment. We all, poor people especially, need good places to live — places where we can live in safety and dignity, and where we have the opportunities and supports needed to build healthy lives and communities. Public housing can meet that need.

Appendix: Methodology

In addition to examining historical and contemporary documentary records, and the rich body of work on urban issues and especially urban neoliberalism, I have relied heavily on interview data — particularly open-ended interviews to learn what respondents themselves considered to be significant — for Little Mountain, Regent Park and Uniacke Square, and interview data plus participant observation for Winnipeg's Lord Selkirk Park. The University of Winnipeg Senate Ethics Committee approved all interviews.

I became involved in the attempt to understand public housing and the poverty typically associated with public housing in 2005, when Nanette McKay, then executive director of the North End Community Renewal Corporation (NECRC), invited me, because of my involvement in Winnipeg inner-city issues, to write a history of Lord Selkirk Park. LSP, built in Winnipeg's North End in 1967 as part of urban renewal, has been plagued for years by the kinds of problems typically associated in the public imagination with spatially concentrated racialized poverty. I wrote a history of LSP for NECRC and have remained actively involved since then, working closely (in a voluntary capacity) with a variety of community workers and residents on the Rebuilding from Within strategy. I have written about parts of this process in three separate editions of Winnipeg's annual *State of the Inner City Report* (CCPA-Mb 2009, 2007, 2005) and in a paper on Aboriginal women in LSP (Silver 2009a), and have contributed to the writing of many internal documents associated with our efforts. In addition to my participant observation, I have been involved in commissioning interviews of various kinds with LSP residents over these years; in every case the interviewing has been done either by residents or by Aboriginal people who have previously lived in or near LSP. These interviewers were Candi Beardy, Elizabeth Bingus, Pam Hotomani, Claudette Michell, Jennifer Seaton and Jake Wark, with the support and assistance of Diane Barron, Janice Goodman, Cheyenne Henry and Carolyn Young.

Early in the process of attempting to understand the case of LSP, I visited Toronto's Regent Park, Canada's oldest, largest and arguably most famous and most studied public housing project. This was the first of five research trips to Regent Park, during the first three of which I interviewed a wide range of community workers and public officials directly involved in Regent Park's massive redevelopment. During my last two trips, in 2009 and 2010, I conducted relatively short interviews with seventy residents — women and men, younger and older, representing many of the ethnic groups now living in Regent Park — aimed at gaining an understanding of their responses to and evaluations of the redevelopment process.

In 2006, I was invited to be a guest speaker at a conference organized by the Uniacke Square Tenants' Association in North End Halifax. I met many knowledgeable people, including residents, community workers and public officials, and decided to include Uniacke Square in a comparative study of Canadian public housing projects. I made three subsequent research trips to Halifax. During my last trip, in May 2010, I hired Donna Nelligan, a long-time resident, parent and activist in that public housing project with whom I had spoken on each previous trip, to conduct in-depth interviews with ten residents of "the Square," including women and men, younger and older, African-Canadian and not African-Canadian.

Meanwhile, Matthew Rogers, my research assistant on aspects of each of Lord Selkirk Park, Regent Park and Uniacke Square, graduated from the University of Winnipeg and left for Vancouver to do a master's degree in community and regional planning at UBC. He suggested that I include Vancouver's Little Mountain Housing in my comparative study. Matt wrote his master's thesis on Little Mountain and continued work as my research assistant, conducting twenty in-depth interviews, ten of which were with current and former Little Mountain residents, and ten with public officials and community activists living in a neighbourhood adjoining Little Mountain. I made one research trip to Little Mountain, in April 2010, and interviewed a number of the public officials and residents that Matt had interviewed.

Chapter 2

The New Urban Poverty and Public Housing

There is, in most large Canadian and American cities, a new form of poverty, a product of the last thirty years. Its causes are often misunderstood and/or misrepresented. This new urban poverty is especially concentrated in large, inner-city public housing projects in Canada and the U.S. — and in large suburban public housing projects in Europe. It is in housing projects in particular that we see its complex character, the often mistaken interpretation of its causes and the resulting deeply flawed policy responses.

The new urban poverty takes a form best described as spatially concentrated racialized poverty. Large, inner-city public housing projects display a complex of symptoms: a high proportion of residents living below generally accepted poverty lines; high rates of unemployment and low rates of labour force participation; low levels of formal education; high proportions of residents who are minorities and minorities of colour; a high rate of single parenthood, disproportionately female-headed; and a particularly high incidence of street gang activity, illegal drug activities and various forms of violence. Public housing projects have come to be deeply stigmatized by these symptoms, seen by the public and the media as areas where regular people should not go, as "outcast" zones, marginalized from the city as a whole. The people who live there typically come to be blamed for these circumstances; some come to accept the blame, to internalize it, and as a result to engage in forms of behaviour that reinforce and fuel the stigmatization and the blame.

Policy-makers typically throw their hands up in despair, saying that these spaces and the people who live there are lost causes. There are no solutions, they conclude, short of bulldozing the area, dispersing the people and starting again. This was the case with urban renewal in the 1950s and 1960s; this has been the case over the past two decades with the large, inner-city public housing projects that arose where "slum" neighbourhoods had been bulldozed in mid-century.

There is a good deal of writing about urban poverty in the U.S. This issue is somewhat less well developed in Canada. The experience in Canada reflects, and in important ways follows, that in the U.S. The growth of neoliberalism — the withdrawal of the state from its social and economic responsibilities and the turning over to the market and the profit motive of ever more state functions — has had a dramatic impact on urban centres, particularly on inner-city public housing projects. Neoliberal policies have undermined public housing in the past thirty years and continue to threaten the wellbeing of its low-income tenants — those who comprise the instance *par excellence* of spatially concentrated racialized poverty. It is a central argument of this book that different policies — ones that run counter to neoliberalism — could build on the often hidden strengths of public housing projects (and their residents), making them good places to live.

Urban Poverty in the U.S.

In recent decades, explanations of urban poverty that focus on the behaviour and cultural attributes of the poor themselves, at the expense of more materialist explanations rooted in the dynamics of a rapidly changing global political economy, have re-emerged (O'Connor 2001; Katz 1989). This cultural turn has a long history, involving the distinction between the "deserving" and "undeserving" poor (Katz 1989): some of the poor are "undeserving" because their behaviour — often identified as being immoral or otherwise negative — makes them the authors of their own misfortune. Although this understanding of poverty has a long lineage, it is in the mid-century work of Oscar Lewis (1961, 1969) and Daniel Patrick Moynihan (1965) that we find the origins of its most recent expression.

Lewis (1961: 30) argued that the poor have cultural/psychological characteristics that lock them into a life of poverty at an early age, and poverty becomes "a way of life that is passed down from generation to generation along family lines." Even if opportunities arise, Lewis argued, the poor cannot take advantage because they are locked into dysfunctional cultural patterns — they adapt to their poverty and accept it as a given; they have feelings of helplessness and dependency; they are unable to defer gratification, for example — that prevent their doing so. This deterministic analysis leads inexorably to the conclusion that the poor will always be with us, because of their own behaviour and values, and thus they are undeserving, a conclusion that has obvious policy implications that turn out to be consistent with the neoliberalism of the past thirty years: there is little point in attempting to solve poverty.

Moynihan (1965) made a similar argument in his influential and controversial study, *The Negro Family: The Case for National Action*, in which he famously found the source of the problem to be "the deterioration of the Negro family," as evidenced by its matriarchal structure. In Black female-headed families, he argued, children, especially male children, were not properly socialized, resulting in a "tangled web of pathology" (they are "lazy," "criminal and disorderly," "immoral") in Black ghettoes. A careful reading of both Lewis and Moynihan finds the roots of their arguments in structural phenomena — in particular an absence of paid employment. But this side of their argument was lost in the easier forms of explanation they highlighted, in which the cause of poverty was the poor themselves.

That the poor, especially the racialized urban poor, are the source of their own grief is a powerful theme in U.S. public discourse. It is perhaps typified by the conclusion of Christopher Jencks (1967: 443), an influential commentator at the time of the Moynihan debate: "The prescription is to change the deviants, not the system." Other influential American scholars aggressively blamed the poor (Banfield 1970, for example). Charles Murray's (1984) argument was not only that the poor were the authors of their own poverty, but also that social welfare programs worsen matters, a conclusion consistent with the emergent neoliberalism of the Reagan years — "get governments off the backs of the people," and do so by cutting social spending.

These arguments are not only consistent with neoliberal ideology but are also easy explanations. They focus on surface phenomena, the behaviour and cultural attributes of the poor and obscure the deeper structural phenomena, especially the dramatically changed character of the labour market and the neoliberal-inspired withdrawal of the state from support for the poor.

Discourses of Demonization

The words and narratives we use to explain the new urban poverty are important because they have policy implications. Yet the words and narratives most commonly used serve more to obscure than to elucidate. This is what Katz (1989: 3) meant when he said in the opening sentence of his important historical study of poverty in the U.S.: "The vocabulary of poverty impoverishes political imagination." Hancock (2004: 19) observed similarly: "Language plays an essential part in constructing inequality in American political culture." When we develop narratives that blame the poor for their own poverty, as with behavioral/cultural approaches, our political imagination is impoverished: we develop policy responses that are deeply flawed; we do not develop the kinds of policy responses that can solve poverty.

There are several reasons for these behaviourial/cultural explanations. One is that those who benefit from the current system do not want to change it. To promote their own interests, they support particular interpretations of events and phenomena. As Watt (2008: 346) argued: "Politics is an arena in which different interest groups seek to establish a particular narrative or version of events as a means to pursue political objectives." If the poor are the cause of their own poverty, then no systemic change is needed — indeed, as Murray (1984) argued, intervention on their behalf only makes matters worse for them.

The poor are not typically the authors of the narratives by which their circumstances are described. They do not produce the images and metaphors that depicted them. They do not control their "collective representation and identity" (Wacquant 2008: 168). Those who do are not only those with more power but also those who usually have no direct knowledge of the poor and their lives. From the outside and with differing interests, they construct a narrative that situates the poor relative to a white, middle-class and suburban way of life taken to be the norm. The urban poor are not part of this norm. They are the "Other." The explanation for their difference, their spatially concentrated racialized poverty, must therefore be that they have individual or ethno-racial deficiencies. Their lives, their neighbourhoods, are a "tangled web of pathology." They are lazy, criminal, disorderly, immoral. Media depictions result in their being "exoticized" (Wacquant (2008: 1) and "Othered"; they become the "undeserving poor."

Poor places are similarly constructed. Those areas inhabited by the poor are seen as dark, immoral and occupied by strangers. Wacquant (2008: 7, 29) calls this a process of "territorial stigmatization" and refers to:

> the weight of the public scorn that is now everywhere attached to living in locales widely labeled as "no-go" areas, in fearsome redoubts rife with crime, lawlessness and moral degeneracy where only the rejects of society could bear to dwell.

Elijah Anderson (1990: 167) adds:

> White newcomers in particular continue to view the ghetto as a mysterious and unfathomable place that breeds drugs, crime, prostitution, unwed mothers, ignorance and mental illness. It symbolizes persistent poverty and imminent danger, personified in the young black men who walk the Village streets.

These are "discourses of demonization" (Wacquant 2008: 271). We demonize, and thus blame, the poor. Katz (1989: 237) describes this as "the peculiar American tendency to transform poverty from a product of politics and economics into a matter of individual behaviour." This follows from C. Wright Mills' (1959: 8) important distinction between those matters that are truly "individual" or "private" troubles and those that are "public issues." Spatially concentrated racialized poverty is a public issue, with identifiable causes rooted in a rapidly changing global political economy, but it is often depicted as an individual or private problem, caused by the behaviour of the poor themselves.

Poverty and Socio-Economic Structure

Another stream of thought, long present in the study of urban poverty in the U.S., re-emerged in the mid-1980s in the work of William Julius Wilson.

In *The Truly Disadvantaged*, Wilson (1987) described the circumstances of the new urban poverty in American inner cities and laid out the basis of a more structural explanation. He did not, quite appropriately, abandon the insights of the behavioural/cultural forms of explanation. But he argued that these behavioural/cultural manifestations of the new urban poverty were responses to, adaptations to, the new material conditions that had emerged in inner cities. Change these material conditions, he argued, and the behaviour and culture will change, albeit gradually (Wilson 1987: 14).

Wilson (1987, 1996) argued that the root cause of the new urban poverty was the changing character of the labour market. The industrial/manufacturing jobs that those with modest levels of education could previously have relied upon to achieve a standard of living sufficient to support a family were leaving U.S. urban centres for the suburbs, the Sunbelt in the deep American south and beyond U.S. borders (Bluestone and Harrison 1982). These were the jobs taken up earlier in the century by waves of African-Americans who migrated from the U.S. South to northern cities in search of better lives (Jones 1993, 1992; Lemann 1991). These manufacturing jobs were replaced by "contingent" jobs — service sector, part-time, low-wage, no benefits, no security, no union (Teeple 2000) — with which it was difficult to support a family. The consequence, according to Wilson, was that large numbers of inner-city residents, especially African-Americans, were without work, and the widespread absence of work produced changes to family structures and a variety of behavioural adaptations, many of them negative.

The character of the "Black ghetto" was, therefore, different in the post-1970 era than it had been in earlier generations. Always segregated, African-Americans had earlier lived in urban spaces that included a full range of occupations and of business and professional services. Although poor, its residents worked and supported a rich array of Black social and cultural institutions (Wacquant 2008; Wilson 1987).

African-American scholars had long identified the importance of the labour market, and of racism, in U.S. urban poverty. W.E.B. DuBois (1899) found that although African-Americans had a higher labour force participation rate than Whites in Philadelphia, they worked in lower-paid jobs, and he identified their segregation, social exclusion and relative family instability — themes resurrected in the last part of the twentieth century — as products of a variety of factors, chief amongst which was the "widespread feeling all over the land… that the Negro is something less than an American" (284). Even at that early date DuBois identified the behaviourial characteristics of the Black lower class that would in the 1960s be seized upon by "culture of poverty" and "tangled web of pathology" interpretations; the difference was that DuBois firmly situated these phenomena in material circumstances, including racism.

In the 1920s, 1930s and 1940s, the powerful Chicago School — urban sociologists at the University of Chicago — saw African-Americans' arrival in the city as subject to a process identical to that experienced by newly arrived European immigrants: a process of competition, conflict and accommodation, or "ecological succession," that was "natural" and that would ultimately lead to assimilation (Park et al. 1925). African-American scholars — Johnson (Chicago Commission on Race Relations 1922); Frazier 1932, 1933a, 1940; Drake and Cayton 1945; Cox 1948, for example — placed a greater emphasis on the role of racism and its deep and lasting effects, and how racism structured the urban experiences and social exclusion of African-Americans.

The post-1960s flight of manufacturing jobs from U.S. inner cities, together with the suburbanization of those who could afford to leave (Jackson 1985), led to inner cities being "hollowed out," worsening the situations of those, disproportionately African-Americans, left behind. Whole neighbourhoods came to be characterized by the relative absence of residents in the labour market. This had a multiplier effect in inner-city neighbourhoods, making it difficult for young people to find work, since doing so had historically been the result of knowing someone, a relative or neighbour, who had a job and who provided job search information and a good word to the boss. The scarcity of people active in the labour market also made it difficult to learn the cultural norms associated with work (Harrison and Weiss 1998). The result was a *Black Youth Employment Crisis* (Freeman and Holzer 1986; also see Neckerman and Kirschenman 1991). With fewer and fewer people working in the inner cities, women, Wilson (1987: Chapter 3) argued, increasingly chose to raise children on their own. What was the point in having an unemployed male in the home? The result was a dramatic increase in the numbers and proportions of inner-city households that were single-parent, female-headed families — what Moynihan (1965) had identified as the *cause* of inner-city problems. Even though he did situate their roots in labour market changes, Moynihan placed the weight of causality on "the deterioration of the Negro family." Wilson, by contrast, placed the weight of the explanation in the dramatic, post-1960s changes in the structure of the labour market, which have been the result of globalization, de-industrialization and neoliberalism.

Wilson's materialist explanation of the new urban poverty, with its focus on the changing character of the labour market and Black inner-city joblessness, inspired a wealth of important intellectual work on the phenomenon (Katz 1993; Jencks and Peterson 1991). Some argued that Wilson had underestimated the importance of "race" (Massey and Denton 1993). Prior to the publication of *The Truly Disadvantaged*, Wilson (1978) had published *The Declining Significance of Race*, in which he argued that for African-Americans, class was now more important than race — as evidenced, he argued, by the upward mobility of middle-class African-Americans. In *The Truly Disadvantaged*, he developed this argument further, emphasizing that growing numbers of African-Americans were trapped in inner cities hollowed out by de-industrialization and suburbanization and that the effects of racism were less the result of currently existing restrictions than of the weight of a racist history, which, when combined with the loss of jobs, became internalized and manifested itself in the behaviourial/cultural forms identified by Lewis and Moynihan. But it was the absence of paid employment, Wilson (1996, 1987, 1978) insisted, that created the "underclass" and the forms of poverty-related behaviour now identified with inner-city poverty.

Still later, Wacquant (2008) argued that Wilson had underestimated the importance of the state. Comparing inner-city Chicago and suburban Parisien *banlieus* — in Europe "inner-city" conditions and large public housing projects are found on the periphery of large urban centres (van Kempen et al. 2005) — he found that while the latter suffered many problems similar to those of U.S. Black inner-city ghettoes, they were not nearly as severe. The explanation, Wacquant argued, was that the French state had maintained a somewhat positive presence in public housing–dominated *banlieus*, mitigating the worst effects of their spatially concentrated racialized poverty, while in the U.S. an historical aversion to the positive state had been severely accentuated by the post-1960s rise of neoliberalism. Wacquant (2008: 3–4) describes this as "the double retrenchment of the labour market and the welfare state from the urban core," adding that "in the final analysis, however, it is *the collapse of public institutions* [his emphasis], resulting from state policies of urban abandonment and leading to the punitive containment of the black (sub-) proletariat, that emerges as the most distinct cause of entrenched marginality in the American metropolis." Venkatesh (2000) described the virtual abandonment since the 1970s, by all levels of the state, of the Robert Taylor Homes, the vast stretch of public housing projects on Chicago's south side that became the poster child for what is largely conceived to have been the "failure" of public housing in the U.S. Others (see especially Newman 1999) argued that Wilson had over-emphasized inner-city joblessness and that in fact large numbers of inner-city residents were working, albeit in "contingent" jobs. These many responses to and elaborations of Wilson's work have deepened our understanding of spatially concentrated racialized poverty and the problems with which it is associated.

Wilson's work has also laid the foundation for a deeper understanding of street gangs, illegal drugs and violence, which have these past two decades been such a central feature of the new inner-city poverty. Hagedorn (2008, 2007), for example, argued that this is a global phenomenon, a product of the global economic change that has produced what Mike Davis (2006: 13, 17) described as "urbanization… radically decoupled from industrialization," resulting in "the mass production of slums," the creation, indeed, of *A Planet of Slums* (Davis 2006: 19).

For the first time in human history, half of the world's population now lives in urban centres (Davis 2006: 1). But unlike the industrial revolution of the nineteenth century, when English peasants were forced off the land and into the "dark satanic mills" of a rapidly industrializing England, the horrifying conditions of which were described by Engels (1987) and countless others, today people throughout the world are moving off the land and into urban centres where they do not work in dark satanic mills. There is almost no wage labour. The resulting conditions are horrendous, and out of these material circumstances, particular forms of behaviour and cultural adaptations emerge, including street gangs, with young men struggling to find a way to make a living in an increasingly jobless but networked world saturated with invitations to enjoy the benefits of the consumer lifestyle.

Adverse material circumstances produce behaviourial and cultural responses. The explanation is not in the behaviour; it is in the conditions that generate the behaviour. It is essential to see beneath the symptoms to find the material causes. Nevertheless, inner-city residents, faced with very difficult material circumstances of inner-city life, do not simply acquiesce. They are resilient and creative; they resist (see Venkatesh 2006; Feldman and Stall 2004; Williams 2004; hooks 1990, for example). A strong sense of community exists in many public housing projects, including those examined later in this book.

These rich debates have yielded a much greater insight into the circumstances of U.S. inner cities than was available prior to Wilson's path-breaking work in the mid-1980s. The causal link between global economic change and especially de-industrialization on one hand, and the emergence of the new inner-city poverty on the other, are clear. So too is the importance of the withdrawal of the state in the era of neoliberalism and the continued effects of racism. Out of this mix emerges, in a complex, non-mechanical way, a variety of behaviourial and cultural responses and adaptations, some negative, others infused with dignity and courage. The cultural and behaviourial character of the new inner-city poverty matters deeply. Lewis and Moynihan and many others were not wrong in identifying inner-city culture and behaviour as an important part of the problem. But they were wrong in seeing it as the root cause and as being unchangeable. Change the material conditions and the behaviour will change too, although not instantly.

Canadian Inner-City Poverty

The study of poverty in Canada has long been plagued by the same individualistic, blame-the-poor explanation that has been so powerful in the U.S. This was the case in Winnipeg's pre–Second World War North End, for example, where Eastern European immigrants who spoke odd languages, dressed differently and ate "smelly" food were called "bohunks," "polacks," "dumb hunkies," "drunkards" (Mochoruk with Kardash 2000: 5–6). Their depiction — by those who rarely if ever ventured into the North End — justified the lack of public investment there that has long characterized Winnipeg's political economy (Artibise 1975). A blame-the-poor discourse, or "poor-bashing" (Swanson 2001), has continued in Canada.

Studying poverty in Canada was rare after the first decades of the century, but the late 1960s and early 1970s saw a surge of interest. This was likely attributable to the radicalism of the 1960s, the sense of optimism about the possibilities of social change, and events in the U.S., including the mid-1960s War on Poverty — the major attempt to eradicate U.S. poverty, which was undermined by the soaring costs of the war in Vietnam — and the 1962 publication of Michael Harrington's influential *The Other America.* The Senate (Canada 1971) and the Economic Council of Canada (1968) produced studies of poverty that said somewhat dramatic things by today's standards. The Economic Council called the high levels of poverty in Canada a "disgrace." The Senate report called poverty "our national shame," said that the social welfare system had "outlived its usefulness," called for a guaranteed annual income and argued: "The system has failed because it has treated the symptoms of poverty and left the disease itself untouched" (Canada 1971: xiii–xvi). A more radical alternative study was conducted, on the grounds that the Senate report had not addressed the systemic causes of the "actual production of poverty" (Adams et al. 1971: v). Edited volumes on poverty in Canada were published (Harp and Hofley 1971; Mann 1970). Much was said in various studies about the invisibility of poverty in Canada (Lithwick 1971: 52; Adams et al. 1971: 1), the absence of research (Lederer 1972: 1–2; Mann 1970: xi) and the fact that poverty in Canada was experienced primarily by elderly, female-headed families and in declining rural regions (Adams et al. 1971: 68; Brewis 1971). The idea of the poor as socially excluded was used in some instances (Economic Council of Canada 1968). Reference was occasionally made to Aboriginal people and the effects of colonization (Harding 1971), but the urbanization of Aboriginal people was only just beginning (Silver 2006a: 13–17), and very little was said about the urbanization of poverty in any event (although see Copp 1974; Lithwick 1971). Little was said about immigration, because the 1967 changes to immigration laws that would result in the dramatic growth in the numbers of "visible minorities" in large urban centres was, like the urbanization of Aboriginal people, just underway. Thus, the racialization of poverty in urban centres was not at all a focus, as it was in the U.S. Spatially concentrated urban poverty was typically mentioned only in passing, with brief references to downtown or inner-city slums ringed by more affluent suburbs (Lederer 1972: 60). Almost all of this work was rooted in a structural analysis of poverty. Mention was frequently made of Oscar Lewis and the culture of poverty (Harp and Hofley 1971; Mann 1970) — indeed, considerable reliance was placed on the much more well-developed U.S. analyses — but Canadian studies emphasized that while the poor may adopt different value orientations, these were best understood as adaptations to their social circumstances, however much public opinion blamed poverty on the poor (Lithwick 1971: 13).

It was frequently mentioned in this late 1960s–early 1970s work that the poverty of the time was a "new poverty," different from that of the 1930s, for example, when most working-class people were poor. By the 1960s, by contrast, most Canadians were seen to be doing relatively well, and the poor were thought to be residual categories of people left out of the benefits of the post-war boom: the aged; those in certain regions, Atlantic Canada for example; the relatively few female-headed families; and Aboriginal people on rural and northern reserves. Occasionally mention was made of African-Canadians, particularly in Nova Scotia (Clairmont and Magill 1970). There was as yet very little about spatially concentrated urban poverty, with the partial exception of Montreal and to a lesser extent Toronto (Gosselin 1971; Urban Social Development Project 1970; Delegran 1970), although in some cases (Lithwick 1971: 18; Delegran 1970) the characteristics of the urban poor that are today more widely known — a high proportion of female-headed families, high rates of unemployment, for example — were identified. It was only in the mid-1980s and especially the 1990s that the image of urban poverty as spatially concentrated and racialized began to emerge.

New Canadian Poverty

This new form of poverty emerged partly in response to dramatic changes in immigration patterns following reforms to Canadian immigration law in 1967, with a tripling of the number of "visible minority" immigrants between 1981 and 2001. This was especially the case in Canada's largest urban centres: the visible minority population increased from 13.6 percent of Toronto's population in 1981 to 36.8 percent in 2001; the corresponding figures in Vancouver were 13.9 percent and 36.9 percent (Balakrishnan et al. 2005: 204–205). Some studies (for example, Ley and Smith 1997) found the emergence of the spatial concentration of poverty but relatively little racialization of concentrated poverty. Hajnal (1995: 514) found: "On one hand race greatly influences one's chances of living in concentrated urban poverty. On the other hand, most people in concentrated urban poverty are in fact white." Others (Balakrishnan et al. 2005; Fong and Shibuya 2000) found a high incidence of both spatially concentrated and racialized poverty in Canadian cities.

> We found that residents of areas with such high levels of spatial
> separation of the poor were mostly members of visible minorities:
> more than 40% of Asians and blacks in Montreal, and nearly 40%
> of blacks in Halifax, lived in areas with poverty rates above 30%....
> in Canada, the spatial separation of the poor from the general
> nonpoor population is confined largely to visible minorities (blacks
> and Asians). (Fong and Shibuya 2000: 453–54)

More recently the United Way of Greater Toronto (2004), for example,
found not only a significant increase in the incidence of poverty in Toronto
between 1981 and 2001 but also that it had taken on a spatially concentrated
racialized character, while Khosla (2003) found a particularly high incidence
of poverty amongst racialized female-headed single-parent families.

Using 1986 and 1991 Census Canada data, Kazemipur and Halli (2000:
7) analyzed the "new configurations of poverty" in Canadian urban centres
that are characterized by "a distinguishable ethnic and racial colour and a
visible neighbourhood dimension" that make "the poverty of the 1990s a
new poverty [emphasis in original], distinct from that of the pre-1960s." They
demonstrate that although the incidence of spatially concentrated racialized
poverty is not as high in Canada as in the U.S. and although it varies considerably by city, the phenomenon does exist, often in association with the
presence of public housing (Kazemipur and Halli 2000: 150, 158; see also
Ley and Smith 1997: 36), and as is the case in the U.S., it produces behav-
ioural/cultural responses consistent with the "culture of poverty" thesis:

> The spatial concentration of poverty is not merely about the geo-
> graphical distribution of a group of people in urban space. It can
> also lead to social and psychological processes with far-reaching
> consequences for the living conditions of the poor. (Kazemipur
> and Halli 2000: 37)

Social and economic inequality in Canada has, to a considerable extent,
become racialized. Galabuzi (2006: xi), who emphasizes "the growing social
exclusion of racialized group members," roots this phenomenon not only in
historical processes but also in global economic restructuring, the emergence
of precarious work and the withdrawal of the state (Galabuzi 2006: 182–86.
See also Lee 2000; Ornstein 2000) and identifies its increasing spatial concentration in urban centres (Galabuzi 2006: 187–90; see also Hou and Picot
2003; Fong and Shibuya 2000; Fong and Gulia 1999). Galabuzi (2006: 189)
concludes: "In Canada's urban centres, the spatial concentration of poverty
or residential segregation is intensifying along racial lines." Again, these
phenomena are rooted solidly in material changes:

Globalization-generated pressures have led to the retreat by the state from its social obligations, leading to social deficits that impact racialized communities disproportionately.... When racialized spatial concentration of poverty leads to racialized group members living in neighbourhoods that are heavily concentrated and 'hypersegregated' from the rest of society, these neighbourhoods become characterized by social deficits such as inadequate access to counselling services, life-skills training, childcare, recreation, and health care services... Young immigrants face a crisis of unemployment, despair, and violence. They are disproportionately targets of contact with the criminal justice system. (189–90)

What Galabuzi describes above as the "retreat by the state from its social obligations" has been deliberately promoted by neoliberal forces in Canada. The Fraser Institute, via the work of Christopher Sarlo, for example, has sought to redefine poverty in a narrow, purely monetary fashion to include only those unable to afford basic physical necessities, the absence of which would jeopardize their "long term physical well being" (Sarlo 1996: 196). Using this narrow and "mean-spirited" (NCW 1998/99: 27) definition, Sarlo (1996: 2) is driven to say, in defiance of the evidence, that "poverty, as it has been traditionally understood, has been virtually eliminated. It is simply not a major problem in Canada." This attempt to define poverty out of existence is consistent with the ideological orientation of the Fraser Institute, which promotes reduced government expenditures on social programs and reduced levels of taxation. And both social program spending and government revenue from taxation have been dramatically reduced in recent decades in Canada. Since the mid-1990s, the three levels of government in Canada have collectively cut taxes by an amount now equivalent to $90 billion per year (Mackenzie and Rachlis 2010: 25), thus dramatically reducing governments' fiscal capacity to spend on social programs. As early as the late 1990s, government spending in Canada as a share of gross domestic product was the lowest it had been since 1950/51 (Yalnizyan 1998: 64). Canada now ranks twenty-fourth out of thirty Organization for Economic Cooperation and Development (OECD) nations for expenditures on social programs (Mikkonen and Raphael 2010: 35). Changes to the Canada Assistance Plan (CAP) led to severe cuts in spending on social assistance — Ontario cut such spending by 21.6 percent in 1995, for example — while changes to the Employment Insurance system cut the level and duration of benefits and dramatically reduced the number of Canadians receiving benefits (Silver 2007b: 204). These and other related changes to social assistance programs in Canada are the tangible expression of the neoliberal withdrawal of the state from its social obligations. They magnify the adverse effects of the new poverty, which is about much more than simply a shortage of income — as debilitating as lack of income is in a money-based society. The new poverty is also about social exclusion, racialization and spatial concentration and is associated with inadequate housing, lack of access to a wide range of services and high levels of crime and violence.

This has especially been the case in large, inner-city public housing projects in Canada, just as in the U.S. (Kazemipur and Halli 2000: 150, 158; Ley and Smith 1997: 36). It is important, therefore, to enquire further into the emergence and character of public housing. There has been a close association over the past thirty years, in fact and in public and academic discourse, between spatially concentrated racialized poverty and inner-city public housing.

Public Housing in the U.S.

Both the *Housing Act* of 1937 and that of 1949 linked public housing in the U.S. to slum clearance. This "virtually assured that low-income housing would be built in distressed, often undesirable, urban locations" (Turbov and Piper 2005: 5). From the 1950s to the early 1970s, tens of thousands of new public housing units, many of them high rise projects, were constructed annually in U.S. inner cities (Bratt 1989: 57). In St. Louis, for example, the Pruitt-Igoe project consisted of thirty-three eleven-storey buildings. The world's largest public housing project, Robert Taylor Homes in Chicago, comprised "a two mile stretch of twenty-eight 16-story buildings containing over 4300 units" (von Hoffman 1996: 433).

These vast, high-rise, concrete projects would become home to the poorest of the poor and to disproportionate numbers of African-Americans. Of the fifty-four public housing projects operated by the Chicago Housing Authority in 1968, 91 percent were located "in areas which are or soon will be substantially all Negro" (Biles 2000: 150). By 1998, of the 11,000 tenants in Robert Taylor Homes, 99 percent were Black and 96 percent were unemployed (Biles 2000: 265). Spatially concentrated racialized poverty and inner-city public housing were virtually synonymous.

Attempts to build public housing outside the inner city, in the suburbs, met with aggressive opposition (Biles 2000: 151; Fuerst 2003: 5). Public housing became a means of confining African-Americans to inner cities, thus "preserving racial ghettos" and spatial segregation (Biles 2000: 150; Hirsch 1983; Crump 2003: 181). Large public housing projects in the U.S. came to be inextricably bound to and closely identified with inner cities, poverty and the racialization of poverty.

The Early Promise

Nevertheless, the evidence is that at first, tenants considered the projects good places to live. Fuerst (2003: 2) shows that from the 1940s to the early 1960s, Chicago Housing Authority (CHA) projects

> helped thousands of Chicagoans escape slum housing conditions and enter a world that offered first-rate housing, a close-knit community, and the positive pride that comes from a shared experience. In short, public housing and the CHA once worked — spectacularly well. (See also Feldman and Stall 2004: 72–78)

Vale (2002) writes that: "In Boston, as in many other American cities… those who gained new apartments were delighted." Radford (2000: 105), referring to the public housing built in the 1930s by the Public Works Administration, said that "Ordinary citizens expressed their approval by moving into the federal developments — even when they might have afforded other accommodations."

By the mid-1960s, this was no longer the case. Large public housing projects were identified with racialized poverty and violence. "To many Americans… public housing had metamorphosed into a dumping ground for society's unfortunates and an absolute last resort for anyone who could not possibly do better elsewhere" (Biles 2000: 152). What caused this transformation?

The Deterioration

From the beginning, private developers, chambers of commerce and politicians opposed the development of good quality public housing; it provided competition to private developers and cut into profits (Bratt 1989: 56; Radford 2000: 105). Thus, most large public housing projects are located in inner cities, take the form of high-rise towers to save on property costs and were poorly built, also to save on costs (see also Turbov and Piper 2005: 5; Popkin et al. 2004: 16; Quercia and Galster 1997: 536, 540).

As the U.S. economy weakened in the 1970s and the global economy began to re-structure, and governments responded with reduced spending, public housing further suffered. It came to be seen as both symbol and cause of urban problems, but the more accurate interpretation is that public housing came to be a receptacle, or "warehouse," for those most badly damaged by the broader changes in the political economy of urban America. The problem is not public housing. As was shown to be the case with poverty generally, the problem is global economic restructuring and the associated emergence of neoliberal governance. But public housing was asked to deal with the worst *effects* of this problem, and in doing so came to be identified with, and even mistakenly seen as a *cause* of, the problem. Public housing has been blamed for problems that it did not cause, but whose victims it was asked to house. And it was asked to do so in rapidly deteriorating inner-city environments and with steadily declining resources.

The demographics of public housing also changed, from two-parent working-class families to larger numbers of social assistance recipients and lone-parent families. This happened because the projects became housing of last resort for those left behind by a rapidly changing global political economy. Fuerst (2003: 199) argues that since the 1970s public housing in Chicago has come to "warehouse" those in greatest need and has become a "modern day poorhouse."

Vale (2002: 6) advances the same argument:

> A half-century before, public housing had valiantly serviced the working poor, but now it struggled to house America's most desperate urban residents. As the 1990s ended, only about one in five public housing households reported earned wages as its primary source of income, and more than three-quarters of households were headed by a single female. Moreover, since the majority of public housing residents were Black or Latino, the program as a whole faced increased political marginality.

Venkatesh (2000: 276), in his analysis of Chicago's Robert Taylor Homes, observes:

> In its first three years, Robert Taylor was a success by any definition, in large part because the CHA and tenants had the freedom and resources to meet household needs. The two parties screened applicants rigorously, mixed working and poor families in the high-rises, and drew on the resources of the wider community to support tenants and decrease their sense of isolation. By the mid-1960s, the deluge of impoverished households that came to the Housing Authority seeking shelter made this conscious planning and social engineering unworkable. Buildings soon became filled with households in poverty, the CHA and organizations in the complex were stretched beyond their capacities.

Families whose incomes rose above a certain level were required to leave public housing. "Access to public housing was thereby restricted to the most economically disadvantaged segments of the population" (Venkatesh 2000: x), unlike the 1960s, when public housing tenants were a mix of income categories (Quercia and Galster 1997: 541, 566).

The very low incomes of public housing tenants reduced the rent revenue available for repairs and maintenance, producing a downward spiral of deterioration: "Caught between rising costs and falling rents, city officials began to cut maintenance and security budgets for the deteriorating projects" (Hoffman 1996: 436. See also Turbov and Piper 2005: 5–6). The Chicago Housing Authority

> neglected basic maintenance, attributing this neglect to lack of federal funds. Working class families with options fled in the early 1970s, triggering a budget crisis that brought about a further deterioration of conditions. A highly predictable downward spiral ensued. (Fuerst 2003: 6)

As the deterioration set in, criticism of public housing mounted. One book "condemned Pruitt-Igoe and other giant projects as human disaster areas" (von Hoffman 1996: 436, referring to Rainwater 1970). Pruitt-Igoe was torn down — dynamited — in the early 1970s, determined by civic authorities in St Louis to be beyond redemption, and seen as evidence of all that was wrong with public housing.

Racism became inextricably linked to the negative perception of public housing projects like Pruitt-Igoe, 98 percent of whose residents were African-American. From the beginning, in 1951, "whites could not be convinced to move into the project." As a result, "moneys for the project began to dry up immediately... money for landscaping and any services (public spaces like gyms, playgrounds, a proposed grocery, even public bathrooms) disappeared." By the early 1970s, "the only tenants who stayed were those with nowhere else to go, most often single mothers with more than four children" (Birmingham 1998: 1, 3, 8).

By the 1980s, the large high-rise public housing projects were dominated by gangs, drugs and violence (Popkin et al. 2004: Ch. 2). Venkatesh (2000: 3), describing the domination by gangs of Chicago's Taylor Homes, quotes a tenant saying: "It used to be our community, but it's theirs now. [The gangs] have taken over." Kotlowitz (1991: x–xi), in his vivid description of the lives of two young African-American boys in Chicago's Henry Horner Homes in the mid-1980s, writes:

> I was unnerved by the relentless neighbourhood violence he [Lafayette, the older of the two boys, then ten years of age] talked about.... And then I asked Lafayette what he wanted to be. "If I grow up, I'd like to be a bus driver," he told me. *If*, not *when*. At the age of ten, Lafayette wasn't sure he'd make it to adulthood.

The book's title, *There Are No Children Here*, arises from a comment made by the boys' mother to the author: "But you know, there are no children here. They've seen too much to be children."

The rise of crack cocaine added to the problem:

> The potential revenue from crack economies escalated conflicts between gangs, and increasingly weapons were used during these disputes, often in public spaces where tenants and their children were present. (Venkatesh 2000: 111. See also Kotlowitz 1991: 38)

The growth in drug-related gang violence coincided with the severe economic recession of the early 1980s. As one tenant in Robert Taylor Homes put it: "People was messed up, wasn't no work.... The young people have nothing to do. No jobs. No recreation. So they are rowdy. They don't go to school. They make trouble." (Venkatesh 2000: 118–19)

The political Right, opposed from the outset to good quality public housing, seized upon the problems with a renewed determination to eliminate public housing. The Reagan administration cut funding to Housing and Urban Development (HUD) by 76 percent from 1980 to 1988 and responded to the inevitable rise in social problems with increased state repression (Venkatesh 2000: 119). The Right waged

> a relentless campaign of individual and territorial stigmatization designed to undermine political support for the [public housing] program.... Widely disseminated media images of welfare mothers living in decayed public housing projects were used to develop a linkage between the morally loaded concept of welfare dependency and the material landscape of public housing. These campaigns helped to convince the public that the only solution to inner city decay and disorder is the demolition of public housing. (Crump 2003: 181)

The growing perception of public housing as warehouses of the poor contributed to the further isolation by race and class, to the spatial and social confinement to the "projects" of those, as well as recently arrived immigrants, and especially Black and Hispanic immigrants (Schill et al. 1998), who have been left out of the American dream:

> No place in the United States, with the possible exception of prisons and certain hospitals, stigmatizes people in as many debilitating ways as a distressed inner city public housing project... these stigmatized individuals have accumulated in environments that themselves only added to the stigma. (Vale 2002: 13)

The result is large, inner-city, public housing projects that are home to extreme concentrations of racialized poverty and that are the breeding grounds for gangs, drugs and violence. The problem is less public housing than the broader forces of a rapidly changing urban political economy, which have left many inner-city residents behind and then warehoused them in public housing long allowed to deteriorate.

That the problem is not public housing as such is made evident by the fact that not all public housing in the U.S. has been a disaster. Public housing for seniors has continued to provide much needed, good quality affordable housing. "Moreover, many thousands were and are content to live in the inexpensive apartments that public housing projects offered, as long as some semblance of personal security was included in the bargain" (von Hoffman 1996: 436). As Naperstek et al. (2000: 3) note: "The great majority of these [public housing] projects are neither large nor distressed. In accordance with HUD mandates, most provide decent, safe, and sanitary housing." And Fuerst (2003: 209) makes a strong case, based on the early experience with public housing in the U.S., that with good management, adequate funding and reasonable screening, "public housing for low-income, female-headed families can be sanctuaries, not penitentiaries."

Public Housing in Canada

In Canada, public housing followed a similar trajectory, although there are not in any Canadian city the vast numbers of public housing units that characterized many U.S. cities. Such project as Robert Taylor Homes in Chicago, with its twenty-eight sixteen-storey buildings, and Pruitt-Igoe in St. Louis, with its thirty-three eleven-storey buildings, are not seen in Canada. Canada lagged behind the U.S. in developing public housing (Brushett 2001: 238) and even now has "the smallest social housing sector of any Western nation except for the United States," with only 5 percent of Canadian households living in social housing (Hulchanski 2003: 3).

As in the U.S., government and business have long opposed public housing in favour of the private, for-profit provision of home ownership, business benefitting from the support of "a well-financed lobby, sympathetic ministers and deputy ministers, and a majority of Canada's voters" (Hulchanski 2003: 5). In 1946, C.D. Howe, perhaps the most influential federal minister of his time, said in the House of Commons: "It is the policy [of this government] to ensure that as large a portion as possible of housing be built by the private sector" (quoted in Sewell 1994: 7). Prime Minister Louis St. Laurent said in October 1947: "No government of which I am a part will ever pass legislation for subsidized housing" (quoted in Rose 1958: 85). Almost all post-war federal housing programs were aimed at home ownership, and at those who could *afford* home ownership, rather than at rental accommodation for those with low incomes (Sewell 1993: 91–92).

Nevertheless, there was in Canada a brief period — between 1949 and 1968 — when large public housing projects were constructed, as part of "slum clearance" programs. The provisions were set out in the 1949 *National*

Housing Act (NHA), which required that the federal government pay 75 percent of the costs and the provinces the remaining 25 percent (Sewell 1994:
133). Under the 1964 NHA the federal government would pay 90 percent
of capital costs, share operating losses equally with the provinces, and leave
ownership vested with the provinces. The 1964 *Act* was a "turning point" for
the development of public housing in Canada: "In 1964 there were about
10,000 units of public housing in Canada; by the end of 1974 that number
had risen to 115,000" (Sewell 1994: 135).

Numerous reports had been published in the period leading up to and
immediately after the Second World War, drawing attention to the "slum"
conditions in large Canadian cities and calling for the removal of "slums"
and their replacement with public housing. "Extensive studies of Halifax,
Hamilton, Ottawa, Winnipeg, Montreal, and Toronto in the early 1930s
showed a proliferation of dilapidated housing conditions, lack of affordable
housing units and rampant social distress" (Purdy 2003c: 52). Vancouver
was no different (Wade 1994). Significant numbers of Torontonians lived in
terrible conditions in emergency shelters after the Second World War, and
"their housing problems epitomized a much larger problem in the city and
across the country — a severe low-income housing shortage for more than
one-third of Canadians" (Brushett 2007: 376). The Bruce Report of 1934
"contains the first slum clearance and rehousing plans for Cabbagetown,
which later became Regent Park" and "soon became the 'bible' of social
housing activists, not only in Toronto, but across Canada" (Brushett 2001:
ix, 105; see also Sewell 1993: 66–72; Rose 1958: 37–45). Its philosophy was
typical of the nineteenth-century-inspired belief — environmental determinism — that all social problems were caused by slums and could be solved with
their eradication: "Only the elimination of the entire slum neighbourhood,
not just the individual slum houses, could mitigate the pathological effects
of slum areas" (Brushett 2001: 110).

Across Canada, areas seen as slums were bulldozed to make way for
public housing. In Halifax, Africville was bulldozed in the 1960s, and
many of its residents were relocated, most ending up in one or other of
two newly constructed North End public housing projects, Uniacke Square
and Mulgrave Park. In Winnipeg, the Salter-Jarvis area, long identified as
a slum, was bulldozed in the 1960s, and on the site Lord Selkirk Park was
built, completed in 1967.

In Toronto, Cabbagetown was razed and replaced in the early post-
war period with Regent Park North (RPN). The design of RPN was typical
of large urban renewal/public housing projects of the time: "Get rid of the
street system; demolish as many buildings as possible; create great chunks
of open space; and build functional structures that looked entirely different
from everything else" (Sewell 1993: 150). The same was the case, albeit on

a smaller scale than Regent Park, with Uniacke Square and Lord Selkirk Park.

In Toronto, a series of urban renewal projects were built between the 1940s and 1960s: Regent Park North and Regent Park South; Moss Park; Alexandra Park; Don Mount (Sewell 1993: 152–55). Each involved the destruction of existing "slum" neighbourhoods and their replacement with public housing. The overall number of low-income housing units was reduced, because more housing was destroyed than was replaced by public housing (Purdy 2003c: 55). This was the case in Winnipeg as well (Yauk 1973). In both cities, large numbers of those displaced moved within a one-mile radius and, in at least some cases, ended up in worse housing situations (Brushett 2001: 340; Yauk 1973).

However, the attempt to do the same in Toronto's Trefann Court met stiff opposition from neighbourhood residents. Sewell argues that "Trefann Court spelled the end of urban renewal in Canada," and led to the establishment in 1968 of a federal task force headed by Paul Hellyer to review housing policy (Sewell 1993: 162; see also Brushett 2001: 35).

Hellyer's Task Force on Housing and Urban Development, whose report was released in January 1969, called for an end to urban renewal, saying famously: "The big housing projects, in the view of the Task Force, have become ghettos of the poor" (Hellyer 1969: 53–54).

The Early Promise

As was the case in the U.S., public housing in Canada was initially successful. In Winnipeg, at Gilbert Park (sometimes known as Burrows-Keewatin), a large public housing project was built in the northwest corner of the city to accommodate those displaced by slum clearance. The *Winnipeg Tribune* (October 16, 1966) reported:

> Social and emotional problems have not disappeared from Burrows-Keewatin. But they are no more severe than in any other community in Winnipeg…. Police seldom visit the development…. They spend less time in Burrows-Keewatin than they do wealthy River Heights. Children play hookey less and do better in school than they did on Jarvis Ave…. Delinquency and crime have decreased. Alcoholism is being controlled. Employment is high.

Regent Park was "hailed as a universal success at the time it was built" and for many years was upheld "as evidence of how the principles of modern planning could magnificently transform the lives of society's poorer members" (Brushett 2001: 42, 98).

Early tenants of Regent Park were happy with their new housing. "In place of a home in often deplorable condition at a rent that took a large portion of the family income, they were moved into a large new apartment with rent based on income" (Sewell1993: 72). Hugh Garner, author of the classic Canadian novel, *Cabbagetown*, writes in the author's preface to the 1968 edition: "The new housing was a godsend to the ex-Cabbagetowners" (viii; see also Rose 1958: 120–21, 134).

Purdy (2003c: 135) adds:

> Early newspaper reports show that people were genuinely pleased with the new spacious accommodations and facilities... More recent oral and documentary testimony gathered by the author confirm these sentiments. Many found the apartments spacious, well kept and in sound condition.

In the early years, Regent Park was largely confined to two-parent working families, particularly veterans. Applicants underwent a personal home visit by a Regent Park staff member, were evaluated on a five-point scale for "Suitability as a Tenant" (Purdy 2003a: 8), and "problem families" — those "whose family relationships, behaviour and moral standards, and standards of housekeeping are so far below the accepted standards that they are judged incapable of improvement" — were kept out (Rose 1958: 205). There were long wait lists:

> Even before RPN had been completed in 1957 there were 7000 applications on file for the project. From the inception of the waiting list for RPS in 1957 to the end of 1959, there were 13,527 inquiries received by the MTHA [Metro Toronto Housing Authority]. By 1959 the waiting list for these units was almost 10,000 names long. By 1970, the Metro Toronto housing registry office had 38 employees to receive 10,000 calls a month and 2000 new applications a month. Applications on file reached 16,000 in 1969 (Purdy 2003b: 465; see also Brushett 2001: 363–64).

This huge demand is evidence of the need that public housing projects like Regent Park were meeting and the relative attractiveness of the housing.

The Problems Now

Within twenty years of its establishment, Regent Park was being condemned as a "new slum," a "colossal flop" (Purdy 2003a: 2). Brushett (2001: 98–99) notes:

> Regent Park became the symbol of all that was wrong with modern planning and public housing: it was too large, too impersonal, too bureaucratic, and was largely alien from the interests of its residents....

By the 1970s Regent Park had returned to the landscape of poverty, crime, and despair that had once marked Cabbagetown in planners' 'bad books,' and had animated their plans for its removal.

In 2002, the *Toronto Star* described Regent Park "as a 'poster child for poverty'" (Purdy 2003a: 2).

The result is that public housing, the housing of last resort for the poorest of the poor, and for a particularly racialized and spatially concentrated form of poverty in hollowed-out inner cities in Canada as in the U.S., became deeply stigmatized, worsening the problems of its tenants.

Yet the problem, as in the U.S., is less public housing than the dramatic changes in North America's urban political economy and the associated rise of neoliberalism, whose victims have disproportionately ended up in public housing because of the paucity of alternatives. "Indeed, after the long economic boom ended in the 1970s, lack of affordable housing has been one of the chief features of the new urban poverty in all advanced capitalist countries" (Purdy 2003b: 471). Rental housing has been in declining supply all across Canada for years. This has been especially the case for low-income renters — those most in need of affordable housing. Kent (2002: 9) has called affordable housing "the greatest of urban deficiencies." Private developers have not invested in low-income rental units for many years because the profits are too low (Carter and Polevychk 2004: 7), and since 1993, the federal government has largely abandoned social housing. Rental housing was 27 percent of all new housing constructed in Ontario from 1989 to 1993; it was 2 percent of new housing built in Ontario in 1998 (Layton 2000: 79). "While construction began on more than 30,000 rental units every year during the 1970s in Ontario, this figure had fallen to approximately 2000 by the end of the 1990s" (Le Goff 2002: 4). The result has been "a dramatic decline in the availability of low rent units" across the country (Pomeroy 2004: 7). There are now long wait lists in most cities for access to social housing (CCPA-Mb 2005: 15; Carter 2000: 5, 11; Hulchanski 2002: 8). In Canada the "ultimate housing problem" (Hulchanski 2002: 17) is the shortage of low-income rental housing. As a recent study by the Toronto Dominion Bank (Drummond et al. 2003: ii) noted: "The overall supply of rental housing in Canada has stagnated in recent years, and has actually been receding at the lower end of the rent range — the segment of the market where lower-income individuals with affordability problems are concentrated." Low-income people least able to find a place to live resort to public housing.

A Design Problem?

A dominant explanation for the problems associated with public housing in Canada, as in the U.S., is design. The argument is that the design of the large public housing projects, influenced by Le Corbusier, has created unsafe conditions (see Jacobs 1961; Newman 1973; Coleman 1985; and Sewell 1993). Jane Jacobs, referring to the urban renewal era, says: "Not to mince words, planners and their working colleagues did not know what they were doing. Their remedies for slums, congestion, and other maladies were frauds" (Jacobs, in Sewell 1993: x). Jacobs et al. argue that the solution is to redesign public housing projects, re-integrating them into the existing street grid, ensuring that units face onto streets and have front and back yards and eliminating pedestrian pathways (Sewell 1993: 228–29).

But this book argues that these design changes deal only with the surface manifestations of the problems of public housing and that a deeper understanding requires an examination of broader societal trends and socio-economic forces. For example, many public housing developments were poorly constructed. Dennis and Fish (1972: 174–75) offer clear evidence that governments deliberately set out to construct low-quality housing that would not compete with private for-profit housing providers (see also Rose 1958: 74; Purdy 2003c: 82). Most public housing was built in inner cities. Public housing did not cause the deterioration; inner cities were "hollowed out" by the powerful forces of suburbanization and de-industrialization. But because so much public housing was constructed in inner cities, whatever its design might have been, it was left to deal with the resulting human problems.

With the shortage of good quality, low-income rental housing, people living in poverty had nowhere else to go. As public housing became home to those most adversely affected by the dramatically changing urban political economy, governments cut spending on repairs and maintenance. A stigma became attached to public housing and to those who were its tenants.

The Power and Danger of Popular Discourse

Adding to the stigma are the ways that low-income urban areas and public housing projects are described in popular discourse. The language — "ghettoes of the poor," "slums" — conjures up images that can drive public policy. Brushett (2001: iii) argues that the process of urban renewal, and its destruction of low-income neighbourhoods "was due, in large part, to the way in which these neighbourhoods were portrayed in popular discourse."

The words used to describe inner-city Toronto neighbourhoods such as Cabbagetown included "cancer," "diseased," "decay," "criminal," "dark," "squalid," "blight," "festering," "immorality." Slums were places of "disease, distress, disorder, disaffection and decay" (Brushett 2001: 15, 3; see also Purdy 2005: 530). This slum narrative came to justify the wholesale destruction of neighbourhoods. In this way, Brushett (2001: 1–2) argues: "Toronto's poor neighbourhoods — slums — were imagined communities," comprised largely of stereotypes, and slum stereotypes were crucial to the advancement of particular political agendas… there were many ways to solve the housing problems of Toronto's poor, but there was only one way to solve the problem of the slum — that is to erase it, to wipe the blots from the face of the city through massive urban renewal and public housing projects which were the most costly solution of all.

The same occurred in Winnipeg. The Salter-Jarvis neighbourhood was the object of blanket condemnation. South of Dufferin was in bad shape; north of Dufferin was a healthy, albeit low-income neighbourhood — what one long-time resident described as "a good area to be poor in" (Yauk 1973: 46). Yauk argues that urban planners looked at the North End from the outside, with middle-class values and no real personal knowledge of the area or its people. Where North Enders saw "a good area to be poor in," urban planners saw only a "slum," "blight," "deterioration and decay" (Yauk 1973: 52). And in the era of urban renewal, the City's response to the serious problems in the southern portion of the Salter-Jarvis area was to apply to the *entire* area "a bulldozer operation lacking both an insight and perception of the slum problem itself" (Yauk 1973: 2).

Nor is this a phenomenon confined to the past. Purdy (2005: 530) argues:

> From the disorderly, Victorian slums of the 19th century to the dangerous "no go" neighbourhoods of today, these slum representations have had a tenacious hold on the imaginations and practices of 20th century urban reformers, the media, state officials and the wider public.

One-dimensional and surface-level depictions of inner-city public housing projects continue to be used as a justification for their destruction, to the disadvantage of their low-income residents.

The Role of Neoliberalism

The on-the-ground, day-to-day difficulties faced by tenants in large, inner-city public housing projects are directly linked to dramatic changes in the global political economy. Neoliberalism has re-shaped the world, including urban centres, since the late 1960s–early 1970s. Neoliberalism involves a series of measures intended to change the role of the state and turn more decision-making authority over to the market — a process sometimes called "marketization" (Peck and Tickell 2007: 35). These measures include privatization, de-regulation, various forms of free trade and cuts in taxes and government spending. The intent has been to free businesses from government-imposed constraints in order to improve their profitability. This has facilitated the globalization of economic activity, a process furthered by changes in computerization and in communications and transport technology.

Among its many effects, globalization and neoliberalism have changed the structure of the labour market in North America, and particularly in the inner cities, and have resulted in cuts in government spending on social programs aimed at the poor (Peck and Tickell 2002; Teeple 2000). Thus, neoliberalism has been a particularly important causal variable in the rise of the new urban poverty. As argued earlier, spatially concentrated racialized poverty is, in large part but not only, a function of: (1) changes in the character of the labour market, especially the relative disappearance of industrial/manufacturing jobs and their replacement with contingent jobs — part-time, low-wage and without benefits, job security or union protections — with the result that large numbers of inner-city people are either working in jobs that pay poverty-level wages or are outside of the labour market entirely; and (2) cuts in government spending, especially spending on social and other programs aimed at those on the lowest levels of the income scale.

Neoliberalism, adopted to a greater or lesser extent by governments of all stripes, has had a major impact on cities. Peck and Tickell (2002) argue that cities are at the forefront of neoliberalization. Senior levels of government have "offloaded" responsibilities to civic governments, including housing in some provinces, with particularly dramatic results, since municipal governments have limited capacities to generate tax revenues (Mackenzie and Scarth 2004). The result has been not only cuts in civic spending but also privatization, user fees, public-private partnerships (Loxley 2010) and an attempt to improve the tax base by attracting both footloose corporations and high-income earners. From this has emerged the "entrepreneurial city, directing all its energies to achieving economic success in competition with other cities for investments, innovations, and 'creative classes'" (Leitner et al. 2007: 4).

This is what Hackworth (2007) has called the "neoliberal city." In the neoliberal city, downtowns and urban cores once abandoned because of suburbanization are now being revitalized and reconfigured, with the result that "the inner city of many large cities is now dominated by toney neighbourhoods, commercial mega-projects, luxury condominiums, and expensive boutique retail shops" (Hackworth 2007: 99). Integral to this neoliberal spatial reconfiguration of twenty-first-century urban centres is the process of gentrification, which takes place at least in part to meet the needs of the kinds of highly skilled and geographically mobile people that the "entrepreneurial city" now seeks to attract. But this same process places at risk such structural legacies of the mid-twentieth-century social welfare state as inner-city public housing projects. Hackworth (2007: 149) argues:

> Gentrification is the knife-edge neighbourhood-based manifestation of neoliberalism. Not only has it created a profit opportunity for real estate capital, but it has also created a high-profile ideological opportunity to replace physically Keynesian managerialist landscapes of old — represented by public housing, public space, and so on — with the entrepreneurial privatized landscapes of the present.

Crump (2002: 582) makes a similar argument: "The demolition of public housing erases from the landscape the highly stigmatized structures of public housing, aiding in the reimaging of the city as a safe zone for commerce, entertainment and culture."

In Canada, this is precisely the risk faced by the low-income tenants of public housing projects located immediately contiguous to or close to downtown areas that city leaders and planners seek to revitalize in ways consistent with the privatizing thrust of neoliberalism. All that is public, including public housing, is at risk; spatial restructuring is designed to serve the interests of the more well-to-do, at the expense of those who are poor. Housing, which ought to be seen as a necessity of life and a human right, comes to be treated like any other commodity, its price rising inexorably beyond the means of the poor, including many of those who are working. This is a particularly dangerous trend at a time when low-income rental housing is everywhere in short supply.

HOPE VI

The severity of the problems of spatially concentrated racialized poverty and public housing in the U.S. led, in 1989, to the creation by Congress of the National Commission on Severely Distressed Public Housing. The Commission produced a national action plan calling for a ten-year strategy "to eliminate severely distressed public housing by 2000" (Turbov and Piper 2005: 7). In response, Congress launched HOPE VI — Home Ownership for People Everywhere — in 1993. It has been described as "a dramatic turnaround in public housing policy and one of the most ambitious urban redevelopment efforts in the nation's history" (Popkin et al. 2004: 1). It is premised on the belief that the high concentration of poverty and unemployment "was a major contributor to the high levels of social problems in distressed public housing." This premise is in a direct line of descent from Wilson's (1987) work on the sources and effects of spatially concentrated racialized poverty. The solution, embodied in HOPE VI, is to deconcentrate poverty by knocking down large public housing projects, replacing them with mixed-income housing with more units sold at market rates, and providing vouchers to displaced low-income tenants, enabling them to relocate to other neighbourhoods. The result has been "a massive demolition and reconstruction effort" (Quercia and Galster 1997: 549). The intention is to create new, healthy, mixed-income neighbourhoods that no longer look like, nor have the stigma long attached to, large high-rise public housing projects.

Much of the discourse around HOPE VI is about improving physical design — a move from high-rise towers to a more garden apartment/townhouse design. In this, HOPE VI embodies the "new urbanism" — a movement among city planners, architects and developers that rejects "modern" planning and takes advantage of the positive impacts yielded by traditional designs. In important ways, the strategy is successful. Turbov and Piper (2005: v), for example, start their analysis of HOPE VI projects by saying:

> Across the United States, attractive mixed-income developments and revitalized neighbourhoods are being created where distressed public housing once stood... the HOPE VI program has converted the nations' worst public housing projects into the foundations of healthy neighbourhoods, providing quality affordable housing while attracting new market activities and radically changing the urban landscape.

In "formerly distressed neighbourhoods" in Atlanta, Louisville, Pittsburgh and St. Louis, Turbov and Piper (2005: v) found that

> household incomes in each of these case study projects grew at a faster pace than that of their city or region, after redevelopment. Unemployment and workforce participation rates have improved. Crime levels have dropped dramatically, as much as 93 percent in Atlanta's Centennial Place. Where revitalization efforts focused on school quality, student test scores dramatically improved... property values and new investments have also soared in these more viable, mixed-income communities.

But the real story is the mass demolition of low-income rental housing. Individual Public Housing Authorities awarded HOPE VI grants are not required to replace all of the public housing units eliminated as part of a redevelopment plan. Most "do not replace anywhere close to 100 percent of the felled units. Only slightly more than half of the units to be built with HOPE VI dollars will be even nominally 'public' (i.e., affordable to the existing tenantry)" (Hackworth 2005: 35). Like urban renewal in the 1950s and 1960s, the total number of low-income rental units is being reduced.

The improved neighbourhoods and reduced crime statistics cited by advocates of HOPE VI may simply reflect yet another occurrence of the historic pattern of "slum clearance" — the poorest of the poor are pushed from one low-income neighbourhood to another. For many, HOPE VI "is another form of 'urban renewal' that is displacing poor households from gentrifying neighbourhoods" (Popkin et al. 2004: 28).

Advocates of HOPE VI argue that housing vouchers enable former public housing tenants to re-locate to higher-income neighbourhoods. However, there is evidence that policies aimed at moving people out of low-income and into higher-income neighbourhoods have not worked as well as first thought. Careful studies of the results have found that those who moved gained little if anything relative to those who remained in inner-city public housing (von Hoffman 1996: 441). Many who used vouchers to move to the private for-profit market are having trouble making their rent payments (Popkin et al. 2004: 30). Middle-class neighbourhoods have generally resisted such programs (Hogan 1996). Oakley and Birchfield (2009: 606) confirm that most families vouchered out of public housing do not experience improved circumstances, but end up in different but still poor African-American neighbourhoods:

> Our findings suggest that the prospects of escaping high-poverty neighbourhoods through relocation are very slim. Even if conditions are improved through demolition of public housing and its replacement with mixed-income housing in the original neighborhoods, these benefits are not attainable for the majority of former public housing families relocated with housing vouchers. Our findings suggest that the primary consequence is that many relocated families will remain in highly disadvantaged neighbourhoods, just not in public-housing facilities.

The destruction and non-replacement of low-income rental units represents the deep flaw of HOPE VI. It is reminiscent of the widespread displacement of "slum" residents during "urban renewal" in the 1950s and 1960s. Those most in need of affordable rental housing will now have even less such housing available to them. As Goetz (2003: 256) puts it:

> A responsible antipoverty policy should not lead with demolition of low cost housing and the forced relocation of the poor. This nation's history with the urban renewal program suggests that without complementary actions to reduce exclusionary barriers and incentives that foster and facilitate growing socioeconomic disparities… the scattering of poor people, in itself, accomplishes little.

HOPE VI is important because, at least in part, it is the model upon which some housing authorities in Canada are basing their policy and expenditure decisions about Canadian public housing projects. HOPE VI appears to be the inspiration for the redevelopment of both Regent Park and Little Mountain, and may serve, it is argued later, as the inspiration for a redevelopment of Uniacke Square in Halifax, in a way disadvantageous to its low-income, largely African-Canadian residents.

While it is clear that HOPE VI is a powerful expression of neoliberalism at the urban level, a complete understanding of any given effort to impose neoliberal policies has to take into account the pre-existing political and economic conditions, and has to take account of whatever forms of contestation that may emerge (Leitner et al. 2007). Thus, we turn to a consideration of spatially concentrated racialized poverty in Little Mountain Housing in Vancouver, Regent Park in Toronto, Uniacke Square in Halifax and Lord Selkirk Park in Winnipeg.

Chapter 3

"It's Prime Land, and Why Would They Leave That to Poor People?"

Vancouver's Little Mountain Housing

Little Mountain Housing in south Vancouver is distinctive among large urban public housing projects in having been a good place for poor people to live and to raise their families. Residents interviewed from 2008 to 2010 were unanimous in making this case; many neighbours in surrounding communities concur. Little Mountain is different in this respect from what we have come to think about public housing projects. Yet, despite having been a healthy community for low-income households, Little Mountain has been bulldozed. It will be replaced on the same site by a mixed-income, mixed-tenure development with a greater density and a high proportion of market

Little Mountain, April 2009, cyclists ride past boarded townhouse through green space near Oriole Walk.
Photo by Matthew Rogers.

housing geared to those with much higher incomes than the original residents. The redevelopment process can be understood in the context of both the dramatic changes in Vancouver since the 1980s, driven in part by the city's integration into global and especially Asian capital and real estate markets, and the neoliberal reconfiguration of the downtowns and central spaces of large urban centres across North America.

The urban poor are the victims of this process. The Little Mountain site, where 224 low-income rental units once stood, now lies vacant. The already severe shortage of low-income rental housing has been made worse. Governments have constructed a variety of explanations intended to justify the redevelopment and to obscure the damage to the poor. But the bulldozing of Little Mountain is a particularly egregious example of what happens when urban land and housing are used as commodities rather than homes and communities. Different solutions were possible, ones that would have improved, not worsened, the severe housing problems facing the growing numbers of low-income residents of Vancouver. These better solutions would have required senior levels of government to invest in the low-income rental housing that for-profit developers will not and cannot produce. They cannot because building low-income rental housing is not profitable. The case of Little Mountain makes clear that the housing problems of low-income Canadians cannot be solved without the provincial and federal governments playing a much more positive role.

Vancouver: Gateway to Asia

Until recent decades Vancouver was a relatively small and quiet outpost on Canada's far western shores. In the mid-1960s it had a "stagnating downtown — measured in terms of low capital investment, empty stores and a relatively declining tax base" (Hardwick 1974: vii). In recent decades and especially since the 1980s, it has undergone a dramatic transformation, becoming a gateway to Asia and the recipient of large inflows of Asian immigrants and capital, among the many results of which has been a downtown booming with residential and commercial construction and the city's emergence as "an exemplary twenty-first-century transnational metropolis" (Hutton 2008: 222; see also Barnes et al. 2010).

Vancouver is now well-integrated into the global economy, including financial and property markets. Efforts have been made by the City and province to market Vancouver, especially to the Pacific Rim, as an attractive site for both mobile capital and mobile individuals with money and/or skills. Much of this capital has been invested in real estate in Vancouver, and real estate has become an engine for the city's economic growth, contributing to its shift from a resource-based to a business/services/finance-based and especially real estate-based economy (Barnes et al. 2010). Vancouver's population has grown, and large areas of the city's downtown have been redeveloped as a part of this process (Mitchell 2004; Punter 2003; Hutton 2008, 1998).

Ley (1987) argues that the redevelopment of Vancouver's downtown has taken two different forms since the 1970s, and that these can be seen by comparing developments on the south and north sides of False Creek. The former, driven by liberal urban reformers elected in 1972 as part of The Electors Action Movement (TEAM), sought to contribute to the building of "the humane city," "the livable city." They expressed such principles as "people before property" and "a common concern for the quality of life in our city." TEAM emerged in the wake of a successful attempt in 1967 to block an urban renewal–style freeway that would have bulldozed an older urban neighbourhood (Hardwick 1974: ix). Ley (1987: 45) argues that TEAM introduced more participatory planning processes and that "neighbourhood interests were commonly favoured in locational disputes." Punter (2003: 14, xvii) describes this as part of the "Vancouver Achievement," arguing that TEAM "had a more considered and sensitive approach to development, advocated more participatory planning practices, and a more inclusive vision for the future of the city."

By contrast, the redevelopment of the north shore of False Creek, started in 1980, was driven by a provincial Social Credit government with a "strong private sector orientation to the project" (Ley 1987: 54). It included the creation of BC Place, with a sports stadium at its centre — an instance of the importance of spectacle and festival in the neoliberal city, described by Punter (2003: xviii) as creating "sites of spectacular consumption" and by Bunting and Filion (2006: 68) as attempts to "package" cities for global consumption.

Mitchell (2004: 40) interprets this as a shift in urban policy in the 1980s "from an ethic of social liberalism [as expressed by TEAM] toward a philosophical and practical framework of neoliberalism." The approach used by TEAM was "rolled back" (Peck and Tickell 2002) by the powerful material and ideological forces of neoliberalism. The city was opened up to offshore developers whose commitment was less to neighbourhood preservation and citizen participation than to the maximization of profit. The purchase of the False Creek North properties in 1988 by Hong Kong corporate leader Li Ka-Shing furthered "the integration of Vancouver into the global property markets" (Hutton 2008: 226) and precipitated massive investments of Asian capital in Vancouver real estate (Ley 2010), which became an important engine of economic development, as it has in other cities.

Real estate development becomes a centerpiece of the city's *productive* economy, an end in itself, justified by appeals to jobs, taxes and tourism. In ways that could hardly have been envisioned in the 1960s, the construction of new gentrification complexes in central cities across the world has become an increasingly unassailable capital accumulation strategy for competing urban economies. (Smith 2002: 443)

Housing prices have skyrocketed as a result, adversely affecting many Vancouver residents, particularly the poor.

The restructuring of Vancouver included dramatic changes in Vancouver's labour market since the 1970s — a shift to the service sector and especially business service jobs, similar to but greater than that experienced elsewhere in large urban centres — driven in large part by inflows of Asian capital and relatively wealthy immigrants, which then drove changes in the city's social composition and class structure, spatial configuration and built environment (Hutton 1998; 2008). For example, at False Creek, previously surrounded by sawmills and "obsolete industries" (Hardwick 1974: 13), arose the waterfront homes of the burgeoning high tech labour force. Older industrial neighbourhoods close to downtown gentrified — the consequence in part of "the rise of a new professional and managerial class produced by the growth of the office district" (Hutton 2008: 233). Land prices rose and the city, increasingly connected to the global economy, was transformed.

Among the results was a series of struggles over space in Vancouver. These led to the displacement of poor people and lower-income residents from their affordable rental accommodations by megaprojects in the neighbourhoods immediately south of False Creek (Hutton 2008: 241), and of older middle-class residents, especially women, from their more well-to-do west end neighbourhoods by rising prices and demolitions. Mitchell (2004: 74) describes these and other such examples as expressions of "the increasing disregard for human relations evident in the drive for profit" — a notion that finds particularly clear expression in the struggle over the redevelopment of Little Mountain Housing.

In the struggle over urban space, neoliberalism assigns desirable urban space to the highest bidders, thus squeezing out lower-income residents and consigning them to less desirable spaces. This is what has happened at Little Mountain. Indeed, Smith (1996) argues that the neoliberal city not only fails to make space for the poor, but includes a form of "revanchism" — a revenge directed against the poor and against those redistributive policies, including housing policies, aimed at supporting the poor, on the grounds that the poor are undeserving and are in the way of the inevitable "progress" that unfettered global capital can bring to an urban centre.

Housing and Low-Income People in Vancouver

This "progress" has worsened what has been a constant theme in Vancouver's history throughout the twentieth and into the twenty-first century: the serious shortage of low-income housing (Wade 1994). The problem has been accentuated in recent decades by Vancouver's economic achievements, which have dramatically driven up the cost of both land and housing (Barnes et al. 2010). The average resale price of a home in Vancouver in 2008 was just under $600,000, the highest in the country (CMHC 2009a: 9). The average rent for a two-bedroom apartment in Vancouver in 2009 was $1400 per month, also the highest, and the vacancy rate was lower, at 1.3 percent, than in any other Canadian city (CMHC 2009b). These costs have created extreme difficulties for low-income households, whose numbers have grown dramatically. Klein et al. (2008: 15) observe: "By any measure, BC has among the highest poverty rates in the country, and the greatest degree of inequality (the largest gap between the poorest and the richest households)." The combination of rising levels of poverty and inequality, a median income in 2006 in Vancouver of $47,000 and the most expensive housing in Canada, has meant "that over 50 percent of Vancouver's labour force earns less than is required to afford a one-bedroom condo in the central city" (Barnes et al. 2010). In addition, rental housing is in short supply. "Because of the high cost of land, it has become virtually impossible to build affordable market rental housing" (CALM 2009). As a result, in 2006 Vancouver had the highest proportion in Canada of total households, renters and owners, spending 30 percent or more of household income on shelter cost, at 37.4 percent (Statistics Canada 2006), and the second highest proportion of households in core housing need, at 17.0 percent (CMHC 2009a: 84; see also Conference Board of Canada 2010). It is not surprising, therefore, that "in this climate of severe housing shortage and high prices, the demand for publicly subsidized housing far outweighs supply — BC Housing, the provider of social housing across BC, had over 13,400 applicants on its wait list in May 2008" (Klein et al. 2008: 20). The 2008 *Metro Vancouver Homeless Count*, conducted on March 11, 2008, found 2660 homeless people in the Metro Vancouver region, up 22 percent from the 2174 identified as homeless in 2005, but the report observed that "homeless counts are conservative estimates and widely recognized as underestimates" (Social Planning and Research Council of BC 2008: 1). A more thorough method, modelled on that used in Los Angeles, found 9196 hidden homeless persons in early 2009 and estimated a total of 23,543 homeless in Metro Vancouver for all of the previous year (Eberle et al. 2009: ii–iv). The dramatic changes in Vancouver since the 1980s that have driven up land and housing costs adversely affect many working-class residents, causing particular damage to the poor and pushing many people on to the streets.

This is the broad context — the use of land and housing as a means of profit-making instead of places to live and the resultant soaring costs of housing, including rental housing — in which to analyze Little Mountain, until recent years a successful public housing project in south Vancouver.

Little Mountain Housing

Little Mountain Housing (LM)opened in 1954, Vancouver's first public housing project. Located in the geographic centre of Vancouver, with Queen Elizabeth Park to its immediate west, it included 224 two- and three-storey units and approximately 800 residents in a physically attractive and spacious park-like, fifteen-acre setting. Unlike most large public housing projects, LM's origins are not in the typical urban renewal strategy of razing inner-city slums and building public housing in their place. Rather, it was the site of former military barracks occupied by veterans — the Little Mountain Squatters Association — immediately after 1945, when Vancouver's chronic shortage of low-income housing had been accentuated by war-time shortages (Wade 1994: 131, 148–49). The result is that LM, unlike most large inner-city public housing projects, has from the beginning been located in the midst of an attractive and stable working-class/middle-class neighbourhood.

Residents of LM have long been satisfied with their housing. A 1959 study of social welfare found that "the great majority of tenants in Little Mountain are pleased with the housing project. Some of them are overjoyed with it. It represents, for most, an overwhelming improvement in living conditions" (Fromson et al. 1959: 134). Unlike almost all other large downtown public housing projects, this satisfaction appears to have persisted. Ten residents and former residents of LM were interviewed in late 2008, late 2009 and early 2010. Four residents of the surrounding neighbourhoods were also interviewed, all of them members of Community Advocates for Little Mountain (CALM) or Riley Park South Cambie (RPSC), or both, along with six government officials with responsibilities related to LM.

Residents were unanimously positive about their experiences living at LM. One resident said: "Oh it's fabulous, it's, it's like the absolute best... it's wonderful to live here... I love it here." A woman who had lived eight years at LM said that "it just felt like a really good, not a small town feeling but just everybody out getting to know each other, saying hello to their neighbours and how you doing, you know those courtesies." Yet another woman, who is Aboriginal and had also been at LM for eight years, said in similar fashion that "some of the very first friends that we made here were some of the nicest people I've ever met in my life," and added: "We were saying how absolutely fortunate we were to live in this little paradise... we're living in such a paradise." A woman who had lived fifty years at LM said: "I was happy to be there, I sure was." A Vancouver city planner said: "It was a pretty ideal place to live... the units were well-suited to families."

Parents said repeatedly that LM had been a wonderful environment in which to raise their children. A mother of four told us: "A lot of the kids that were here, they had a sense of belonging, this was their neighbourhood and they felt proud to be here, and when a kid feels a sense of belonging and they've never had that before, they don't want to lose that." She added: "I feel like it's been a really safe place to raise kids." A twenty-year-old man who had spent his entire life at LM concurred:

> Like, I know everyone who lives in this complex... like in the sum-
> mer I'd always go outside and just shoot hoops with a bunch of my
> friends out on the court... I've done so much in this complex that,
> like it's, I couldn't ask for more growing up here, put it that way.

He added: "For me, I would want to raise my kids here, like this was the ideal place to be raised as a child, you know."

Of particular note is the strong sense of community that existed at LM, a view expressed by everyone with whom we spoke. A woman with three children who had been at LM for eight years said: "Oh it's been great. The whole community spirit, we have lots of close friendships and... it was a real nice mix, sort of a community feel."

Residents actively created the sense of community. A woman in her fifties who had grown up in LM and moved back to look after her aging mother said: "I grew up with the example, not just in my house but in the site here, of you don't just point out what the problems are and point a finger and say whose fault it is. You identify the problems, then you look for ways to solve that problem, and then you be part of the process to create that solution." She added: "Mom would volunteer us out to any of the seniors who needed help. I mean, that's the kind of community that it was.... People took care of one another." A resident who has lived near but not in LM for thirty years and who works in Queen Elizabeth Park and thus has long had a first-hand view of life in LM said: "You have a few key individuals who are really into building community and they establish a kind of tradition, and as [new] people come," they adopt and carry on that tradition. Ellen Woodsworth, city councillor for the area, said about LM: "a lot of renowned social activists have lived here."

One of the fifty-year residents had been active with the tenants' associa-tion, which started in 1971 and continued to the mid-1980s. She said that it had two committees: one was the health and welfare committee, "which was responsible for sending out get-well cards to people that were sick, visiting in hospital and if there was a death, sending flowers and so on"; the other was the recreation committee, which she headed for many years, "and the recreation committee was responsible for the activities on the Development." These included hootenannies, sports days with races and trophies, an after-school homework club, a pre-teen group for "our young people and they ran their own meetings… there was always an adult present…. We had 'blacktop dances' where we swept the blacktop off and hooked up some music and the kids danced, you know, and yeah, there was always an adult in charge." In the early 1970s the community realized that "a lot of our kids couldn't swim and they couldn't afford to go to a pool because it was too expensive for swimming lessons," so the community organized to demand that their kids be offered free swimming lessons. "We took a busload down to the Parks Board… we were in the Council Chamber five minutes, they approved the program."

She told another story of flooding a local skating rink, and the first time, "I think I was the only stupid mother that got up at 5 o'clock in the morning and froze her butt off over at Riley Park Ice Rink." A handful of kids joined her "so when we were going home that day I said to the kids, next week you tell your mom and dad or your brother or your sister that they have to bring you. Well, come Sunday morning I started across the Development, this door opens and out comes father, this door opens, out comes mother, this door opens, out comes brother. So I wasn't alone that day…. Yeah, we had a lot of fun in those days, yep." This community-mindedness appears to have become a part of the culture of LM, as opposed to the "culture of poverty," with its characteristic sense of despair and hopelessness, described by Oscar Lewis (see Chapter 2).

Many of those who came to LM did so after negative experiences with housing elsewhere. One woman said: "I had spent two months in a home-less shelter, for god's sake." Another said, in describing previous experience in the private rental housing market: "It was a racial problem that we had, even trying to find a place after I left that place I had to go into the open market for a year," and "I've been asked if I was an Indian on the phone." A woman originally from El Salvador said, about the private rental unit in which she had lived prior to coming to LM: "I come from a small country, but I never see in my country, like, mices in the middle of the night… very dirty."

Little Mountain by contrast was characterized, everyone agreed, not only by a strong sense of community and of citizen engagement but also by a sense of pride in the appearance of the complex. A person who has lived near but not in LM for the past thirty years said: "The place was always clean, you know. You never had a sense that this was like an impoverished ghetto."

Further, unlike most large, inner-city public housing projects elsewhere, LM was relatively crime-free. A woman who had lived at LM for three years was asked if she worried about crime in the neighbourhood: "No I don't, I've never worried about it." Her two children, then fourteen and sixteen years of age, walked home "at like 1: 30 or 2: 00 in the morning, and they came home unmolested, you know.... and I'll be outside smoking a cigarette at 1: 00 in the morning or something like that and everything will be quiet." A woman who had lived twenty-two years at LM said: "I always felt safe when I came in here. I felt safe here. I've always felt safe here." An eighteen-year resident said: "You don't feel worried or scared or anything like that." There was very little street gang activity and related violence at LM. "We don't have gangs that flock together and are selling on the corner here like they are in other projects. We don't have that." She added: "We're all neighbours, you know, a lot of us share the same values, and we really care about our neighbourhood and the environment that our kids are playing in, so we make sure that that kind of stuff doesn't happen here." A woman who has lived five blocks from LM for more than twenty years said: "There were no more gangs in Little Mountain than anywhere else, I would say probably less, you know."

The lack of crime and the strong sense of community appear to be connected. One former resident said that the lack of crime contributed to the sense of community because "that promoted a sense of well-being, you know, getting to know your neighbours. If every second person you live beside is a shady character, right, you're really not inclined to want to open up." The strong sense of community contributed to safety; the relatively high level of safety contributed to the strong sense of community.

Residents said that they felt somewhat stigmatized by outsiders because they lived in a public housing project. One respondent, for example, said that "there was a lot of stigma when our kids were growing up because, oh, they live on the housing developments, you know, they're poor kids, they're on welfare." Another added, when asked if there is a stigma attached to living at LM: "Oh yeah! There is. I learned that by going to school and riding the bus. I'd hear people as we're going, getting up to here [LM], talking about the people that lived in here, like they knew. And it wasn't nice." But the implication of this comment is that people attaching a stigma to LM did not, in fact, have any personal knowledge of LM or its residents. Another said: "Our current minister of housing talks about negative stereotypes of affordable housing and yet I doubt that he's even set foot here nor spoken to one person who lives here." The implication is that any stigma attached to LM and its residents arose from stereotypes, rather than from a real knowledge of the people who lived there. This is the norm with public housing.

Stigma notwithstanding, it appears that the problems typically associated with inner-city public housing projects — street gang activity, crime and violence, social isolation, absence of citizen engagement, for example — were largely absent at LM. There was some youthful gang activity in the

1970s, according to long-time residents, but it never became anything like the problem that has plagued so many inner-city public housing projects in recent decades.

In fact, it is striking the extent to which residents of LM said that the public housing complex was a wonderful place to live and to raise a family. The ten residents and former residents were unanimous in saying that they loved living in LM, that it was safe, that people got along well together and supported each other and looked after each other's children, and that it was a good place to raise a family. While it was certainly home to low-income households (see Table 3-1), it was not the site of the kind of behaviour that has come to be associated with so many large inner-city public housing projects.

Two main questions logically follow: why was Little Mountain Housing a good place to live and to raise a family; and given that it was a good place to live, why was it torn down and redeveloped?

What Made Little Mountain a Good Place to Live?

Three inter-related factors stand out in explaining the success of Little Mountain Housing. First, although the residents of LM were always poor, a higher proportion of residents were in the paid labour force or on seniors' or disability pensions and a lower proportion were on social assistance than is typical of inner-city public housing projects, and there was considerable residential stability. Second, LM was not part of urban renewal and thus was not built on the ruins of a razed "slum." And third, it was well integrated into the surrounding community, which is not a "slum" but a stable working/middle-class neighbourhood. The greater degree of residential stability contributed to a strong sense of community, which was accentuated by the skills and hard work of a number of community activists, whose efforts were important in actively building community.

The Socio-Economic Composition

A senior Vancouver city planner observed that LM had never become the "housing of last resort" and home to the poorest of the poor that is so often the case with inner-city public housing projects. BC Housing ran a "fairly tight shop" in terms of entry requirements, keeping it "relatively trouble-free." LM had long been home to people living in poverty, but its socio-economic characteristics were different from the typical inner-city public housing project, as shown in Table 3-1.

LM was similar to most large public housing projects in having a high proportion of female-headed, single-parent families and very low average incomes. But it differed in having a relatively high proportion of residents earning employment and public pension incomes and a male labour force

Table 3-1 Selected Indicators: Little Mountain Housing, 1981–2006

	1981	1986	1991	1996	2001	2006
Income less than $15,000	—	—	69%	68%	68%	54%
Income less than $25,000	—	—	92%	88%	89%	82%
Female household heads	65%	76%	76%	79%	78%	79%
In receipt of employment income	—	—	43%	38%	36%	50%
In receipt of pension &/or disability income	—	—	39%	45%	47%	40%
In receipt of social assistance income	—	—	50%	57%	51%	40%
Resident more than 6 years	35%	40%	42%	48%	46%	55%
Resident more than 10 years	—	15%	17%	22%	26%	26%

Source: BC Housing. Housing Connections. Adapted from data extracts provided by A. O'Neill, IT Branch, March 2010.

participation rate (67.9 percent) only slightly lower than the rate for the city as a whole (72.0 percent). LM was a low-income community in which a significant proportion of the population worked, albeit very likely in low-paid and/or part-time and/or intermittent jobs, and in which a larger than typical proportion of the population were seniors and/or people with disabilities. Residential stability was fairly high: in 2006, more than half of residents had lived in LM for six years or longer; more than a quarter had lived at LM more than ten years. Residential stability was greater in LM than in Vancouver as a whole and greater than the adjoining middle-class neighbourhood of Riley Park (Statistics Canada 2001). A woman who had lived at LM for more than fifty years said: "Most of the people there were there for years, ten, fifteen, twenty years, thirty years." Several said LM was the place at which they'd lived longest. "This has been the longest we've lived somewhere, so I think it really helped develop a sense of security for the kids, you know." Another added: "No problems with landlords, no problems with other neighbours, it's a place I've stayed the longest in my life." Especially in recent years, the relatively high rate of residential stability was likely attributable not only to the fact that LM was a pleasant place to live, but also to the high cost of housing everywhere else in Vancouver. Even though rents rose with income — the result of the rent-geared-to-income (RGI) rental rate system — residents of

LM were likely to have concluded that they were better off staying than facing the uncertainties of a tight and costly private rental market.

The Character of the Surrounding Neighbourhood

Also atypical of most large, inner-city public housing projects, LM had not been an urban renewal project, had not been built in a bulldozed "slum" neighbourhood and had not located in the midst of a broader "slum" neighbourhood. It was the link between slum clearance and public housing that, from the beginning and in most other cases, "virtually assured that low-income housing would be built in distressed, often undesirable, urban locations" (Turbov and Piper 2005: 5). But as was observed more than half a century ago: "The important feature of Little Mountain as a low-rental "rehousing" project is that it is *not* (emphasis in the original) part of a direct slum clearance program" (Fromson et al. 1959: 33). LM was built in a working-class neighbourhood that has had no experience of spatially concentrated racialized poverty. Riley Park, adjoining LM, is now a "pretty solid middle-class, maybe upper-middle-class neighbourhood," recently affected by the dramatic rise in Vancouver housing prices, said one government official. One nearby resident said that he bought his house in 1980 for $50,000, and "I calculate that at the height of the market a year ago, say, it has gone up fifteen, sixteen times what we paid for it."

Also, Riley Park has been "very neighbourhood-minded, you know," as one long-time resident put it, and this found expression in a remarkable level of community support for social housing in the neighbourhood. This was confirmed by the eighty feedback forms arising from two meetings organized by the City in the neighbourhood in December 2009. According to the City planner in charge of the redevelopment of LM, the feedback revealed that "there is almost unanimous support for social housing on the site, which suggests to me that they [LM residents] were considered good neighbours…. Only two people expressed opposition to social housing." There appears to have been a greater degree of concern about LM expressed by surrounding neighbours in 1981 (Olsen 1981: 19) than was the case more recently, suggesting that relations between LM and its neighbours improved over the past thirty years — exactly the opposite of what has been more typical of public housing.

Integration with the Surrounding Community

LM, unlike most large inner-city public housing projects, was not cut off from but rather largely integrated with the surrounding community. Children from nearby neighbourhoods played with children in LM. One mother said: "Kids that live in surrounding neighbourhoods, their parents feel very comfortable in [their] coming over here. They don't have to worry about them. There's lots of space for them… I was really proud of that." A woman who grew up at LM said that kids from off the complex "would come over here and play here and they'd use the big field at the end over here, the boys would play baseball, football, soccer." Adults interacted as well. Said one: "On the other side here is Quebec Street and we have quite a few friends that we've made throughout the years that live on these streets here… we invite them to our barbecues and our corn roasts that we put on in the neighbourhood… like we see a lot of neighbourhood folks, you know, come in here and sitting around in here and chilling with the people." People in surrounding neighbourhoods regularly walked through LM: it was not seen as a dangerous place, an "outcast space." According to a long-time resident of an adjoining neighbourhood, there were no "invisible walls": "compared to other public housing projects in other cities, [where] a project will often become an island within the city, and the neighbours across the street will not enter, whereas it's very 'porous' here." The Major Projects Planner with the City of Vancouver, responsible from the City's side for the redevelopment of LM, said about the residents of LM:

> They're generally seen as part of the community and they're very active in the community too. I mean, like I said there's a lot of cross-memberships between different groups and there's a lot of people who have come from LM who are involved in the neighbour-hood house, are involved in the community planning processes and stuff like that. They're not distinct in any way. They've blended together.

This appears to have always been the case. In 1959, Fromson observed: "It was encouraging to find, increasingly as acquaintance developed, how large a contribution to the School's PTA has been made by mothers from the Little Mountain families." Seven of twenty executive members of the neighbouring General Brock School Parent-Teachers Association (PTA) were from LM, and of the 200 members of the school's PTA, then known for its well-attended meetings, an estimated 70 percent were from LM (Fromson et al. 1959: 49, 89).

The Issue of Design

The commonly expressed view that the *design* — the removal of the street grid; the absence of through streets; the wide-open spaces — causes social problems in public housing projects (Coleman 1985; Newman 1973) is belied by the experience at LM. Residents appear to have particularly appreciated the design of the housing project, especially the wide-open spaces. Residents and former residents repeatedly made comments such as: "Well, it's like liv-ing in a park, really," and "I love the fact that there is so much green space." All commented positively about the wide-open space at LM and said that children used it constantly to play and parents could watch them from their windows. One person who has lived near but not in LM since 1981 said that "part of the reason I think is because it's on a beautiful piece of land... with lots of places for kids to play."

However, all of the housing at LM was either two- or three-storey units, as opposed to the towering high rises of the Robert Taylor Homes, Pruitt Igoe and parts of Regent Park, and this was a positive design feature of LM, as was the relatively low density. Yet residents' appreciation of the wide open spaces and the absence of through streets, that have in other public housing projects been seen as the cause of problems, suggests that the problems with public housing are not the result of design, or at least not wholly so. As a senior government official put it: "Design is not the sole determinant of social outcomes."

Little Mountain is important because it demonstrates that public housing can provide a good home for poor people. It can provide good quality, inexpensive housing in an attractive physical setting that is safe and healthy, that is conducive to the creation of a strong sense of community and that is recognized by tenants as a good place to raise a family. This flies in the face of popularly held, negative notions about public housing, which have been used in recent decades and continue to be used to justify its tearing down and redevelopment. If LM was not torn down and redeveloped because it was a bad place to live, then what is the explanation?

Why Is Little Mountain Being Redeveloped?

The transformation of Vancouver's economy over the past quarter century has led to population growth, changes in social composition, spatial configuration and the built environment, and pressure on downtown land. Housing prices have skyrocketed, pushing residents ever further from the downtown and creating serious commuter and environmental problems. There is little land left in Vancouver on which to build housing for a growing population.

However, there is Little Mountain, fifteen acres of prime real estate. It is a signature site: physically beautiful; twenty minutes on the new Canada Line Sky Train from downtown and, in the opposite direction, from the Vancouver airport; located in an attractive and stable middle-class neighbourhood; close to amenities. BC Housing (Hemmingson 2008) promoted it as "Vancouver's Premier Redevelopment Opportunity"; a senior BC Housing official called it "a prime location in the city of Vancouver"; and another senior BC Housing official said: "Little Mountain is a gem in so many ways, and it's unique because of its prime location in the city. I mean, wow, what a location!"

These depictions of LM are about its exchange value, not its use value (Logan and Molotch 1987). Little Mountain could produce more money.

A Vancouver city planner said the Province "looked at the piece of land" and thought "they could realize a lot of the value in the land by doing other things with it other than leaving it as it was as a low density public housing project."

Residents of LM were fully aware of this. One said:

> You know what it is, is that they don't want humble people, average people, in the most desirable neighbourhood in Vancouver, okay? They want this land, this piece of land is very desirable, it's next to the most beautiful park in Vancouver and it's in the most desirable neighbourhood. The government looks at it as prime real estate… it's prime land, and why would they leave that to poor people, you know? Like it's too rich, it's too rich, the land's too rich.

In early 2007, the federal government, which had owned it for fifty years, turned the LM land over to the Province. Within months it was up for sale. The provincial government's rationale was that they would "unlock the value" in this prime real estate, that is, they would realize the profits from the sale of "Vancouver's Premier Redevelopment Opportunity" (Hemmingson 2008). Doing so was consistent with their neoliberal ideological orientation. As one CALM activist put it: "We have a provincial government that is just obsessed with the idea of privatizing everything that is public."

BC Housing entered into a Memorandum of Understanding, under which the City agreed to do the following: replace the 224 low-income rental units on a one-for-one basis (as opposed to the 20 percent of units more typically set aside for social housing in Vancouver); offer existing tenants the right of return; increase significantly the density of the site; and use half the profits from the sale of the land to support social housing in Vancouver and the other half to support social housing outside Vancouver (Vancouver 2007).

In 2008, the Province selected Holborn Properties as the developer, but the particulars of the sale and the redevelopment were not known at the time of writing, because as a City plan, the deal

> is confidential between the developer and the Province. So we [the City] don't know anything about the value of that land deal, what the expectations are in terms of timing, density, anything like that.

What is known, according to a senior BC Housing official, is that "part of the contract that we actually have with the buyer of the property, the developer, is a clear and vacant site." This means that, before the sale is finalized, all of the tenants must be removed and their homes demolished, the rationale being that if they were not removed, tenants might continue to resist the redevelopment, and if they were removed and vacant buildings were left standing, squatters might occupy the buildings. So despite the severe shortage of low-income rental housing, the buildings were bulldozed. Only then, after the removal of almost all existing tenants, were consultations about the redevelopment begun, and these consultations were not with residents of LM — they were gone, relocated — but with residents of the surrounding community.

Little Mountain residents, therefore, had no real input into the fate of their community and their homes. BC Housing claimed they used a "residents first" policy, which included the following features: nobody was forced to leave; a relocation office was set up on site in March 2007 to assist tenants in finding new accommodations; free busing was provided to the children of relocated tenants who wanted to continue attending the same school; and vouchers were provided to those unable to find suitable housing in the public sector to enable them to find subsidized private housing. But in reality residents were simply told that they had to move; there was no consultation with them about the future of LM.

Many residents had wanted a phased redevelopment, so that those who chose to stay would not have to leave the site. "If they were truly wishing to be respectful of the people… they [the tenants] have been urging the government to do phased construction and on-site relocation… as the new buildings are built, move us from the old to the new," said one long-time resident. Another added:

> When the whole redevelopment thing started, we realized how prematurely they were moving tenants, and we just felt like that was really wrong because we know that the redevelopment wasn't going to happen until after the Olympics. We wanted to phase it in, because there's a lot of really vulnerable people, a lot of disabled people, some of the elderly that have been here for a long time.

A phased relocation was technically possible. A Vancouver City planner said: "Yeah, it was quite logical and in fact sites like this are often done in phases, it's very common…. You could keep a third of the site occupied while doing demolition…. If you look in the 2007 [City] Council report it recommends that phasing be used as the approach to the site" (see Vancouver 2007).

But there was no phased process. That would have violated the terms and conditions of the sale of the land from the Province to Holborn Properties, which required that a clear site be delivered. The participatory planning and resident engagement that had come to characterize Vancouver was made impossible by the terms and conditions of the sale of the property, i.e., by its privatization.

Prior to December 2009, neither tenants of LM nor residents of the surrounding community were informed of the redevelopment plan. Residents of LM mentioned this repeatedly and angrily: "BC Housing has never, ever consulted tenants [about] what they like or what they wanted. They have been corrupt"; "They haven't been involving the people at all. No, not at all, not at all. From the get-go. I mean we had to learn from the newspaper that this was happening"; "The first that we heard about it was a year ago, we got this, you know, slip of paper through the door saying to visit the relocation office because Little Mountain was going to be torn down"; "They didn't tell us in advance, it was just all of a sudden, you know, you guys are going." Some felt, contrary to what BC Housing said was the case, that tenants were pressured to relocate. One woman referred to "people knocking on my door, coming to me saying, you know, I'm being pressured really badly... Some went through a lot." She added: "What the government does, they instill fear in the people, and they get what they want in the end. They get their prime land, and I mean it's just like the same thing that's going on in third world countries where they're taking land... I just hate the way they've done this, you know, they could have done it much more civilized."

Neither was the surrounding community consulted in a meaningful way. Said one resident: "There's been two times in two years they've sent out a brief one-page description of the status of the project.... We've asked to meet with the developer several times, but the developer refuses to meet with the RPSC [Riley Park South Cambie]." A City planner said: "There has not been very good communication from the Province or the developer on this particular project.... From what I understand the community made a lot of overtures to the Province to try and get dialogue started on this... and did not have letters returned and phone calls and stuff." Another resident of the surrounding community said: "I've been sort of struck by Vancouver, which at the municipal level is so well-known for its participatory planning and its process of engagement, how at this project, which has been handled at the *provincial* [emphasis in the original] level, there seems to be very little process for engaging residents, for engaging the community."

The whole process generated a great deal of anger, both for what was done — the bulldozing of low-income housing when it is in such short supply in Vancouver — and the way it was done, the lack of meaningful consultations with those whose homes were being destroyed. One resident said: "I think the provincial government should be taken and shot, free of charge, because of the fact that social housing, there's so little of it, why take this one away." One member of CALM argued that BC Housing "sold" this unilateral, top-down process to the public with claims that they were replacing the housing at no cost to taxpayers, and profits would be produced for further social housing, and that existing tenants would have right of first refusal in the new units. But "in the process the community was destroyed."

A Conflict Looms

Only in December 2009, when the LM site had been almost completely cleared, did the City begin to hold public meetings with the surrounding community. But the participants in this consulting process were not the residents of LM — they had been relocated. Those participating were the residents of the surrounding community, and they had the opportunity to make their voices heard, not on whether LM was to be bulldozed or not, or whether a phased process of redevelopment ought to be used, but rather on what the new, redeveloped LM site would look like — what would be the character of the redeveloped site, particularly its density and therefore the height of the buildings. The surrounding community said, in interviews and in *RPSC Community Vision* (RPSC 2005), that they were prepared to accept a densification of the redeveloped LM site, but with a maximum height of four storeys. They indicated that they may be prepared to compromise, since a uniform height may not be aesthetically pleasing, but as one resident said: "I think there will be a horrific resistance to, you know, 12-storey, 15-storey towers or more than that." A City planner added: "There's also some feeling out there that the expectation for density [by the developer and the Province] is beyond what would be tolerated, that could be tolerated by the community [and also the City has] our own urban design expectations for the site in terms of what we believe is compatible with the neighbourhood." The Province and developer — whose interest is to maximize profits — no doubt want a density that will require that buildings considerably exceed four storeys.

The surrounding neighbourhood is highly skilled. They are organized in the RPSC Vision Team and in CALM, which in turn is a member of both RPSC and the Citywide Housing Coalition. RPSC has held neighbourhood consultations and prepared a community vision document (RPSC 2005). CALM has engaged in more activist initiatives — "Stand for Housing" events every Saturday for two years, for example, and submissions to City Council, meetings with the developer and art projects on boarded-up LM homes — in support of the residents of LM. Said a Vancouver City planner: "These people are very savvy when it comes to planning and have a good sense of what they want in the area and they don't want. It is very sophisticated. So you can't expect them to roll over on anything."

As important as this conflict is, and as skilled as the surrounding community is, the main battle has already been lost. Little Mountain has been bulldozed and its residents scattered. Few if any will come back. The redevelopment will take too long — at least two years from December 2009 for community consultations and re-zoning. Construction will not start before December 2011, and if it were to start then, completion of the new buildings would take at least a year, to December 2012. No low-income tenants will live at LM before that time.

But the land could lie vacant for longer still. If the surrounding community is successful in preventing the developer from increasing the density to the extent necessary to produce the desired profits, the developer may choose not to proceed at all. Importantly, at the time of writing, the property had not yet actually been sold: "There's been a deposit paid from what I understand. But, from what I've heard the sale doesn't actually take place until the rezoning is complete."

Failure to complete the re-zoning to the developer's satisfaction, or, depending upon one's perspective, success in preventing a level of densification unsatisfactory to the surrounding community, would mean an even longer delay. The LM site could lie vacant for years, even a decade — in a city in which there is a desperate shortage of low-income rental housing.

A Lost Opportunity

The redevelopment of LM could have been worse. In the U.S., the one-for-one replacement requirement was eliminated in 1996 (Wright 2006: 126) and the net number of low-income rental units has been dramatically reduced. At LM the 224 units will be replaced, albeit after what will be an unconscionable delay, and BC Housing has promised that 50 percent of the profits from the sale of the site will be invested in social housing in fourteen other sites in Vancouver.

But the promise to invest profits in social housing sometime in the future may not be fulfilled: governments change, and a new government may not feel bound by the promises of its predecessor; governments break promises that they themselves have made, justifying it on the grounds of difficult fiscal circumstances. Because there is little public support for social housing for poor people, governments may not worry that such a broken promise will hurt their election prospects. Further, the profits are not likely to be invested in subsidized housing for low-income families; they are more likely to be directed to housing for particular populations: those with mental or physical disabilities or addictions, for example (BC Housing 2009). It appears that BC Housing is no longer in the business of providing subsidized housing for people whose only problem is low income. The meaning of "social housing" has changed; it now effectively means "supported housing." People who are poor because their wages are low or because they are outside the paid labour market will have increasingly fewer housing options.

The number of social housing units for low-income households at LM could have been doubled or tripled as part of the redevelopment. Middle-income, affordable housing could have been built, including co-op housing. Or as acknowledged by a senior City official, the buildings, at least many of them, could have been renovated in 2009 using federal fiscal stimulus dollars, as was done at Lord Selkirk Park in Winnipeg. The councilor for the area stated:

> The Province has proceeded by strangling the City into an agree-
> ment and forcing the people out of the housing... dissipating a really
> vital community and in so doing has also left a lot of people on the
> streets homeless at a time when there was a federal program, an
> infrastructural program that they could have applied to rehab those
> units. (Woodsworth, January 14, 2010)

This was not done, and an opportunity lost, because the land on which the
public housing was located has been sold to a private, for-profit developer,
who operates on the basis of profit maximization. Little Mountain and its
erstwhile residents are victims of the social and spatial reconfiguration un-
leashed in the past three decades in a Vancouver now fully integrated into
global and especially Asian capital and real estate markets, where urban land
and housing are mere commodities. In this material and ideological environment, LM is a commodity too valuable to be left to the poor.

Profits Before Shelter

The most important conclusion to be drawn from the LM experience is that
large urban public housing projects can create a good living environment
for poor people. Residents were unanimous in describing LM as a good place
to live and to raise a family. The problems typically associated with large
inner-city public housing projects were not serious issues at LM. There was
some stigmatization from outside, but residents were consistent in saying that
the stigma arose from the stereotypes in the minds of outsiders and not the
reality of day-to-day life in LM.

Second, it is crystal clear that bulldozing LM is a product not of its
unsuitability as a place to live, but on the contrary, of its attractiveness to
those with money, who have emerged victorious in this struggle over space
in the neoliberal city. Little Mountain, in neoliberal terms, is too valuable
to be left to poor people. Large profits can be made by selling the property
and erecting housing for higher-income people. The disposition of the site
and the people who lived there has been decided by what is most profitable,
rather than what is most needed. As senior City of Vancouver officials have
acknowledged in interviews, it would have been possible to double or triple
the number of subsidized housing units on a redeveloped site and to add a
mix of affordable and co-op housing. The destruction of LM is a victory for
those who see urban property and housing as exchange value rather than use
value — as a commodity rather than necessary shelter. It represents a loss
for low-income people struggling to find adequate housing in a city where,
as Barnes et al. (2010) observed, over 50 percent of working people do not

earn enough to own a one-bedroom condo in the central city, where the high cost of land has made it "virtually impossible to build affordable market rental housing" (CALM 2009), and where poverty and inequality are as high as or higher than anywhere in Canada (Klein et al. 2008). One person we spoke with said, "There were many alternatives to what they've done," but the choice that was made was dictated by the neoliberal ideology that *assumes* that the market and the profit motive produce the best decisions for all. She added: "I think it's criminal; it's criminal to allow it to happen."

Chapter 4

"Because It's Not *About* Creating New Housing!"

Contradictions and Limitations in the Redevelopment of Regent Park

Toronto's Regent Park, Canada's largest and oldest public housing project, is being bulldozed and redeveloped in six phases over what will be a fifteen-year period or longer. In large part what is happening is another case of gentrification in pursuit of the creation of the neoliberal city in downtown Toronto. Higher-income homeowners have begun the process of moving into the market units in the redeveloped Regent Park, where they will form the new majority in what was once one of Toronto's lowest-income public housing neighbourhoods. The commitment to replace low-income units and to implement the Social Development Plan makes Regent Park at least potentially different in some important respects from most HOPE VI cases in the U.S. But the expenditure of $1 billion will result in no net gain in the

Regent Park, old and new, on the edge of downtown Toronto, as seen from the fourteenth floor of the new seniors' building, May 2010. Photo by Jim Silver.

number of social housing units at Regent Park and in fact a net loss of such units on the actual footprint. And although the Toronto Community Housing Corporation and the City of Toronto have promoted some progressive community development initiatives as part of the redevelopment, their character is complex and contradictory. In any event, they are not likely to be sustained for long enough to overcome the spatially concentrated racialized poverty that has long characterized Regent Park.

While the redevelopment of Regent Park is in large part another case of the promotion of the neoliberal city, it is in some respects more complex than that. It also includes elements of a place-based anti-poverty strategy. But the challenges associated with the anti-poverty component of the redevelopment are many. There are reasons to fear that few poor people will benefit and that those who have lived the longest in Regent Park will not benefit at all. There are also good reasons to be concerned that the initiatives undertaken at the front end of the project will not be sustained over the long term. This is significant because the deep poverty that has characterized Regent Park for decades is not susceptible to quick fixes. There are only long-term solutions. The process of "social development" is complex and contradictory and the results uncertain.

However progressive or otherwise may be the efforts of local levels of government and government-supported housing corporations, the absence of a national housing strategy, and the neoliberal inclinations of which that absence is a part, place extreme limits on what is possible in the redevelopment of large, urban public housing projects like Regent Park. When seen in this broader context, the redevelopment of Regent Park is likely to be, at best, another case of a lost opportunity; at worst, it may mean the loss, for many of those who have lived longest in Regent Park, not only of a home but also of a sustaining, supportive and much-loved community. The expenditure of $1 billion with negative outcomes for the poor is another instance of the failure of neoliberalism.

The Origins and Early Years of Regent Park

Housing activists prior to the Second World War decried "slum" conditions in cities across Canada and called for their removal and replacement with public housing. A 1911 report found housing in the area that included Toronto's Cabbagetown to be "a menace to public health, a danger to public morals, and, in fact, an offence against public decency" (Hastings 1911: 4). The 1934 *Bruce Report*, the "bible of social housing" (Bacher 1993: 10), "contains the first slum clearance and rehousing plans for Cabbagetown, which later became Regent Park" (Brushett 2001: ix). The philosophy of the *Bruce Report* was typical of the nineteenth-century belief, known as "environmental determinism," that all social problems were caused by slums and could be solved with their eradication. As Brushett (2001: iii) argued, the destruction of low-income neighbourhoods "was due in large part to the way in which these neighbourhoods were portrayed in popular discourse":

> All too often Toronto's working class neighbourhoods were viewed through the lens of the "Victorian slum" and universally portrayed as landscapes of disease, despair and degeneracy — both physically and morally. The inability of Toronto to move beyond a kind of "Victorian environmentalism" to comprehend the diverse realities of inner city neighbourhoods led to the physical and social destruction of much of working class Toronto.

From this way of thinking about low-income neighbourhoods was born urban renewal.

Cabbagetown, deemed a "slum" by urban planners, was razed and replaced in the late 1940s and 1950s with Regent Park (RP), Canada's oldest and largest public housing project and part of an urban renewal program modelled on that in the U.S. Little respect was paid to the people who lived there: "the destruction of Cabbagetown and its renewal as RP was both brutal and authoritarian" (Brushett 2001: 99). Other public housing projects followed, each involving the bulldozing of existing "slums" in downtown Toronto and their replacement with public housing that was physically distinct from the character of the pre-existing neighbourhoods and that included the elimination of the street grid system and the setting of buildings in the midst of wide open spaces. However, the attempt to do the same in Toronto's Trefann Court met stiff opposition from neighbourhood residents. Sewell (1993: 162) argued that "Trefann Court spelled the end of urban renewal in Canada" and led to the establishment in 1968 of a federal task force, headed by Paul Hellyer, and its famous assertion that public housing projects "have become ghettoes of the poor" (Hellyer 1969: 53–54). No more public housing was constructed.

As in the U.S. (Fuerst 2003), public housing in Canada was initially successful. RP was "hailed as a universal success at the time it was built" and for two decades was widely upheld "as evidence of how the principles of modern planning could magnificently transform the lives of society's poorer members" (Brushett 2001: 42, 98).

Yet within twenty years, RP was condemned as a "new slum" and a "colossal flop"; by 2002 the *Toronto Star* called it a "poster child for poverty" (Purdy 2003a: 2). What explains this transformation? As argued previously, the problem was less the design, as many maintain, than the dramatically changed social composition and the curtailment of public funds for maintenance and social development. In common with other public housing projects in Canada and the U.S., RP was initially home to White, two-parent, working-class families, especially veterans. Screening of tenants at RP was tough; limits of 15–20 percent were placed on the proportion of residents on social assistance (Purdy 2003b: 461–65). In its early years, RP was a working-class community, with socio-economic and demographic characteristics similar to Toronto as a whole.

This began to change in the 1960s. A gap emerged between the characteristics of tenants in RP and residents of Toronto generally (Purdy 2003a: 3). Incomes in RP dropped relative to the rest of the city: from 1970 to 1990, average family incomes in RP South dropped to less than half, and from 1980 to 1990, average wages in RP North dropped to less than one-third (Purdy 2003a: 17). The gap in unemployment levels between RP and Toronto similarly widened, as did the proportion of tenants on social assistance (Purdy 2003a: 19–20). The proportion of single parents grew from 7 percent in the late 1950s to 17 percent in the mid-1960s and more than 50 percent by 1981 (Purdy 2003a: 12). Because of a shortage of both low-income rental housing and daycare, and discrimination against women in the labour market, those "most needing public housing were mother-led families and those on social assistance, which explains the particular social composition and abysmally low incomes of tenants in the project" (Purdy 2003a: 33). RP became housing of last resort for the poorest of the poor.

The marginalization and social exclusion of people of colour meant that they too came to be disproportionately represented in RP. Prior to the 1970s, most RP residents were of Anglo-Canadian origin; in the 1970s and 1980s, large numbers of Caribbean and Asian newcomers resorted to public housing. From 1971 to 1986, while the proportion of Blacks in Toronto doubled from 2.5 to 5 percent, the proportion living in public housing grew more than six-fold, from 4.2 to 27 percent (Murdie 1994). The proportion of RP residents born outside Canada was just under 20 percent in 1961; by 2001 it was 60 percent (*Globe and Mail,* April 2, 2005), and some eighty-five languages were being spoken in Regent Park (Milgrom 2003: 228). RP was home not only to the very poor but to the racialized poor and can be seen as an example of the racial production of space (Razack 2002).

Simultaneously, funding was cut, starting in the 1970s, by governments that were "always penurious, half-hearted supporters of public housing," while changes in the global political economy shifted manufacturing jobs out of downtown Toronto:

> [In] 1949, 1953, and 1961… numerous Regent Park North residents worked at large industrial establishments, which would be gradually caught up in suburban industrial decentralization and high contraction and plant closure rates from the 1950s to the 1980s… the locational shift and contraction or loss of large, unionized, and

relatively well-paid manufacturing industry employment in postwar Toronto limited the possibilities of finding well-paid work close to the downtown Toronto location of Regent Park, especially with the majority of families in the project unable to afford a car. (Purdy 2003a: 32)

By the 1980s, the decline in the numbers of jobs in the RP area and the dramatically changing demographic and socio-economic characteristics of RP residents made drug-related opportunities more attractive for growing numbers of young males outside of the labour force. Increased crime, violence and street gang activity resulted, adding to the stigma attached to RP and its residents:

> Condemned as too large and badly designed by academics, as a haven of single mothers, welfare families, and deviants by governments and the media, a magnet for crime and drug problems by police and law and order advocates, and the site of potentially explosive "racial" problems by many popular commentators, Regent Park had come full circle in the public mind from the "ordered community" of the 1940s. (Purdy 2003a: 34)

And as was the case in large U.S. projects, RP youth came to feel confined to their public housing project, limited in the opportunities open to them.

> The streets surrounding Regent Park... marked not only the physical but also the ideological boundaries of Regent Park for many young people, beyond which a different world resided. Considerable research on identity formation among inner city youth has found that ideas about employment, education, and relationships with other groups are crucially shaped by internal spatial contexts such as neighbourhood. (Purdy 2003a: 35--36; see also Purdy 2003c: 34–35)

The voices of RP tenants reflect that feeling. The mother of a youth who lived in RP and was shot and killed in 2001 said: "No one cares what happens to a boy like my son. Everyone judges you when you come from Regent Park. They make you feel like a piece of shit. That's how they made my son feel, and that's how they made me feel." A young woman added: "You can feel like there's no way out. It overwhelms people, and takes away their energy" (*Globe and Mail*, April 2, 2005).

The result is that public housing, the housing of last resort for the poorest of the poor and for a particularly racialized form of poverty in hollowed-out inner cities in Canada as in the U.S., became deeply stigmatized, worsening the problems of its tenants, and contributing to the association between public housing and street gang-based, drug-related violence. All of this occurred in the era of neoliberalism, with the state increasingly unwilling to take the steps necessary to address these problems.

With cuts in public spending, RP was allowed to deteriorate, largely as a consequence of neoliberalism's opposition to public housing and disregard for the poor. By the turn of the twenty-first century, RP buildings were in poor repair. Derek Ballantyne, former CEO of the Toronto Community Housing Corporation, and John Sewell,former mayor of Toronto, both indicated the cost of renovating would likely have been as much as building anew. For years, residents of RP had demanded action to redevelop their community. "People have never been happy with the condition of the housing, the chronic neglect," said one long-time community worker.

All of these material and representational factors — the dramatically changing demographics of RP; its production as an outcast, racialized and stigmatized space; the disappearance of manufacturing jobs; the diminution of the state as a positive force; the emergence of the illegal drug trade and the negative activities associated with it — occurred simultaneously in RP, creating a "perfect storm" that produced the quintessential home to spatially concentrated racialized poverty.

In 2005, following the stillbirth of previous redevelopment efforts in the 1980s and 1990s (Milgrom 2003: 230–51), the current redevelopment began. For the most part it started when it did and in the way it did because an opportunity was seen to "clean up" a stigmatized neighbourhood and make profits by redeveloping it.

The Redevelopment of Regent Park as a Neoliberal Project

In the U.S., the demolition and redevelopment of large, inner-city public housing projects has served the interests not of their low-income tenants but of developers and those who see a sanitized downtown as a strategic part of the creation of the neoliberal city (Hackworth 2007). Crump (2002: 582) argues that "the demolition of public housing erases from the landscape the highly stigmatized structures of public housing, aiding in the *reimaging of the city* [emphasis in the original] as a safe zone for commerce, entertainment and culture." The replacement of public housing is "intended to re-engineer the class and racial structure of the city by bringing middle-class European-Americans back to the inner city" (Crump 2003: 185) — a process identified elsewhere as the "new urban colonialism" (Atkinson and Bridge 2005: 2) and for many years as gentrification.

This is what is happening in Toronto, where the "competitive city" is being planned (Kipfer and Keil 2002) and most of the downtown has been colonized by higher-income residents (Hulchanski 2007). RP is an aging remnant of the Keynesian past, i.e., of the post-war era, prior to neoliberalism, when the state intervened for positive social and economic purposes. It no longer fits with the sanitized and privatized landscape of urban neoliberalism (Hackworth 2007).

In a speech in March 2005 — titled "Unlocking the Value in Toronto's East Downtown: The Revitalization of Regent Park" — Dr. Mitchell Kosny, then Chair of Toronto Community Housing Corporation (TCHC), said: "Rebuilding Regent Park will be a true partnership between TCHC and the private sector... and *we are now open for business*" (his emphasis). The area around RP "has been experiencing an impressive economic rebirth... and the development opportunity is obvious" (Kosny 2005). Not surprisingly, a tenant reportedly said, echoing more recent comments by tenants of Vancouver's Little Mountain Housing: "They're tearing down Regent Park because rich people want the land" (*Globe and Mail*, April 2, 2005).

Given the U.S. experience and that of the residents of Little Mountain, this was a reasonable assumption. In the U.S., public housing has been bulldozed and replaced with a mixture of market, "affordable" and low-income, rent-geared-to-income (RGI) units, with a sharp reduction in RGI units, thus worsening the shortage of low-rent housing (Hackworth 2007; Crump 2003; Vale 2002). Benefits accrue to developers and higher-income people, not to low-income tenants. Fraser et al. (2003: 418) noted: "Urban restructuring and the development of inner-city neighbourhoods may be viewed as arenas where developers, realtors, lending institutions, and a host of other private ventures extract profit and instigate a particular vision of the city." This is precisely what happened at Little Mountain, although the case of LM is slightly less negative than the U.S. experience in that BC Housing made a commitment to replace all social housing units. And this is what is at risk of happening at Uniacke Square in Halifax. A constant discourse of stigmatization of RP has paved the way for this outcome.

Yet in the case of RP some positive elements have been included in the redevelopment process. As well, residents have long wanted a redevelopment of some form, and many residents, although certainly not all, feel positively about the redevelopment and optimistic about their own and the community's futures.

Regent Park Redevelopment: Simply a Case of Gentrification?

Residents of RP have long wanted and struggled for redevelopment but not the dramatic reduction in RGI units typical of HOPE VI in the U.S. In 2001, two long-time residents of and community workers in RP who attended a HOPE VI conference in Toronto said: "We were actually quite shocked with what had happened, and we said we can't let this happen in this community."

The TCHC is committed to a one-for-one replacement of RGI units, setting RP apart from the more destructive U.S. experience, where the one-for-one replacement rule was abandoned in 1998 (Wright 2006: 127). However, the issue of the replacement of RGI units is complex.

First, not all the new RGI units will be located on the RP footprint. The initial plan was that 1770 of the 2083 new RGI units would be on the footprint, with the balance in adjoining neighbourhoods (TCHC 2007b: 23). This has created suspicions that displacement is occurring: tenants are being removed from the RP site and from its sense of community and multiple supports. The new RP will have a much higher density, and a significant majority — perhaps 70 percent — of residents will not be low income. Those relocated to the off-site buildings will no longer be a part of RP.

Second, the TCHC's commitment is to replace all the RGI units by the end of the redevelopment, fifteen years or more hence. However, as one community worker said: "There will be inevitable pressure to increase the number of market units and decrease the number of RGI units." The outcome is likely to be a function of how much pressure RP residents and community-based organizations and their supporters can place on the TCHC to meet its commitment.

Third, and most tragically, after an anticipated $1 billion investment in RP, the best result is the same number of RGI units. Despite the investment of vast sums, Toronto's massive shortage of low-income rental units and a long wait list — 67,000 in April 2008 (Kosny 2008) — the number of RGI units will remain unchanged. The massive net loss of RGI units that characterizes HOPE VI — "in Chicago, demolition of public housing has resulted in the overall displacement of more than a hundred thousand African-American public housing residents" (Hagedorn and Rauch 2007: 448) — will not be replicated in RP, but the expenditure of vast sums with no net gain in the number of social housing units, and in fact a net loss on the RP footprint, represents a colossal failure.

The failure to increase the number of units is a consequence of thirty years of neoliberalism. RP was not adequately maintained during an era of government spending restraints and therefore had to be replaced. None of this would have been necessary "if you bloody well had maintained it in the first place," as one community worker who grew up in RP put it. Governments said that they did not have the funds to finance replacement units in an era committed to tax cuts and expenditure constraints. Thus, public lands were sold to private developers — who make their profits with market units on that valuable downtown property — in order to raise the capital needed to replace the RGI units. The redevelopment of RP is taking the form of a public-private partnership; the land will no longer be publicly owned and controlled. Neoliberal policies led to this public waste and loss.

The Limits of Social Mix

The redevelopment of RP will be an instance of social mixing. Where once RP was home to spatially concentrated racialized poverty, it will upon redevelopment be home to a mix of low-income and much greater numbers of higher-income, non-poor households. Much is made of the merits of social mixing in the redevelopment of public housing. The TCHC, for example, asserted: "Research shows that mixed-income communities can have a positive impact on opportunities and outcomes for residents from all backgrounds" (TCHC 2007a: 2).Yet the evidence that this is so, and in particular that mixed-income housing will benefit low-income tenants of public housing, is weak.

Some studies of social mix in public housing have found benefits, especially in improved safety and better school performance for children, although these are not dramatic (Rosenbaum 1995; Rosenbaum, Stroh and Flynn 1998; Rosenbaum, Reynolds and Deluca 2002; Briggs and Turner 2006).

More substantial is the evidence that social mix strategies produce few if any benefits. A classic study (Sarkissian 1976: 234, 243) found "little empirical evidence" of benefits from social mix and criticized it as a physical/design solution to a social problem. More recent studies call the evidence of benefits from social mix "thin and contradictory" (Atkinson 2005: 20), "thin and mixed" (Musterd and Andersson 2005: 767) and "inconclusive" (Kleinhaus 2004: 384). Allen et al. (2005: 20, 52) conclude that "claims made in relation to mixed tenure are probably exaggerated" and that "social mix is not the panacea for the broad range of social problems that some suggest." Other studies (Joseph et al. 2007; Allen et al. 2005; Popkin et al. 2000; 2004) generally concur.

In particular, evidence does not support the argument that mixed-income housing will produce interactions among different social classes, thus generating the networks that Harrison and Weiss (1998), for example, argue are vital in securing employment in neighbourhoods of concentrated poverty. Allen et al. (2005: 8) "were only able to find one instance where unemployed households had found work as a result of informal help from a neighbour." Joseph et al. (2007: 386) conclude: "Most studies have found little interaction across income levels, and those that have found evidence of interaction have not been able to demonstrate that the interaction has led to information about jobs or other resources." Others have come to similar conclusions (Slater 2005: 53–54; Rose 2004: 284; Popkin et al. 2004: 390). Rose (2004: 281) goes one step further, arguing that the promotion of inclusive neighbourhoods may be aimed more at improving the image of cities than at improving social equity and that the desire to enhance a city's image — for example, to attract the "creative class" extolled by Florida (2002) — may lead to further repression of the poor (Smith 1996).

It is clear that social mix *alone* does not solve problems associated with concentrated poverty. Joseph et al.'s thorough evaluation of the social mix studies concluded that "it is unlikely that mixed-income residence by itself can promote observable change in the short or medium term" and added that "fully addressing poverty among low-income residents of mixed-income developments will require serious investments in education, job readiness, training, and placement" (2007: 399). Public investment in education and jobs is essential. Simply moving higher income residents into RP will, by itself, produce few if any benefits for those who are poor.

But the redevelopment is more than just social mix. It includes an attempt to implement a place-based, anti-poverty strategy, rolled out in the form of the Social Development Plan (SDP). That there is such a plan is notable; how successful it will be in combating poverty in RP, and even whether it is in fact an anti-poverty strategy, is debatable.

According to a senior City planner, no previous developer in Toronto has been required to comply with social objectives, although this has for two decades been the norm in Vancouver (Sandercock 2006: 53–56). The SDP has teeth: City approvals for physical construction are on hold until the provisions of the SDP and the Community Facilities Strategy have been met (TCHC 2007b: 24). There is an apparent commitment to the social side of the redevelopment. The consultant hired to conduct a community engagement exercise said about the head of the TCHC: "He came to me and said... the way we view this is it must be physical redevelopment and social revitalization; if we don't succeed at both we have failed."

The SDP has been designed and will be implemented by three bodies: the Regent Park Neighbourhood Initiative (RPNI), a community-based organization (CBO) that is intended to represent residents in the social development process and that has taken on the role of a social planning body; the TCHC; and the City of Toronto. The result is a large and complex social planning exercise that may make the redevelopment of RP more than simply a case of gentrification.

Yet there are grounds for skepticism. Other large inner-city public housing redevelopments that have made initial claims about social benefits have not only reduced the number of RGI units but also largely failed to meet their commitments on social benefits and resident engagement (Bennett et al. 2006).

The Challenge of Community Engagement

The redevelopment of RP began with what appears to have been a relatively effective process of community consultation. That there was any consultation at all with residents prior to the redevelopment sets it apart from, for example, the cases of Chicago (Smith 2006: 116–17), and Little Mountain. The TCHC hired consultants "to engage a broad swath of the population," and according to one of them, "what they said is get people involved, make sure that they are part of the decision-making." Approximately thirty residents were hired and trained as "animators," people who had skills and were part of "robust social networks" in various ethnic groups in RP (see also James 2010: 80). As one of the consultants described it, the animators conducted the consultations: "They were the ones who designed the engagement process... they were the ones who did the initial interpretation of the data, they were the ones we went back to test the conclusions that we generated based on the data that they gave us." The process included door-to-door conversations and community meetings. Data were gathered, "and then we'd go back to all the animators and say you know this is what we think you told us. Did we get it right? And they'd always say no, and we'd always have to make a bunch of revisions." The entire process was designed to be participatory and culturally appropriate and to get deeply inside the various communities that constitute RP, and to see RP through their eyes. The result was what a senior City planner, who started working in RP in the early 1980s, described as a process of " resident engagement that was qualitatively different from any discussion that had happened previously in Regent Park" (see also RPNI 2006: 2). It is undoubtedly the case, according to a long-time community worker, that some residents felt left out of the process and that the degree and character of participation did not meet the high standards set by Arnstein's (1969) famous ladder of participation, by which "full participation" requires that residents make decisions. The TCHC and the City of Toronto, however much they may have listened to and accommodated the expressed interests of residents, still maintained the authority to make decisions, and did so. Yet, as Milgrom (2003: 3) observed, the involvement of residents is always a difficult challenge, and "in Regent Park the test is even more demanding because, over the last twenty years, the neighbourhood has come to accommodate an unusually diverse population." Add to this the cynicism that has not surprisingly grown in RP because of the constant "consultation" and previous failed attempts at redevelopment. Meagher and Boston (2003: 5) found that "a history of disappointments... has resulted in a predominant mood of distrust and disengagement." Sahak (2008: 54–55) quotes Trina, a long-term resident of RP: "When I was younger, we used to see researchers come by all the time taking surveys and doing interviews like we were animals that needed to be studied." It is clear how difficult participatory decision-making actually is in RP.

Negotiating the Social Development Plan

The consultations resulted in a set of principles (City of Toronto 2005: Appendix One), which then drove the creation of the SDP, the details of which were worked out in three-way discussions between the City of Toronto, the TCHC and the RPNI. "We have sat down almost every week and gone through each chapter, and reviewed those chapters quite extensively, almost line by line," said a senior City planner. The TCHC provided funding to RPNI to enable it to participate in this process, and it has thus been able to play, however imperfectly, the role of a community-based social planning body.

In the early stages, it was believed that residents were engaged in the process:

> It isn't perfect. But I think there's been a really critical shift in terms of saying we're listening to the community... and there's been an enormous amount of effort put into community capacity building, and that almost feels like a catch phrase at this point but enabling the community to articulate its needs, enabling the community to build its own programs.

Yet the RPNI soon became less the voice of the community than a technocratic body disconnected from the community and negotiating in bureaucratic fashion with the TCHC and the City of Toronto. The RPNI board identified the problem and in late 2009 hired a long-time resident as a "community coordinator," assigned the task of engaging the community.

But community engagement has now become exceptionally difficult. "The community" is fragmented, especially along ethnic lines, and is in a constant state of flux, with 380 residents relocated at the start of Phase 1, some of those recently returned after three years, others moving to one of the three off-site locations, and still others not returning at all. Relocations for Phase 2 were starting in May 2010, while newcomers of a different social class have been moving into the new market condos in RP in growing numbers. Engaging "the community" in this state of fragmentation and flux is a challenge: " a very tough row to hoe, a hard slog," as the new community coordinator acknowledges.

Transformation, not Amelioration?

The goal, say the architects of the redevelopment, is grander than community engagement. It is to go beyond the amelioration of poverty, to being "transformative," to creating the structures and opportunities for people and the community to move out of poverty while staying at RP. The intention, said Derek Ballantyne, former CEO of the TCHC is

> to provide community health. Now community health is a number of things: it's housing in a good state of repair; it's opportunities to participate in the civic realm; it's access to services; it's obviously economic welfare and wellbeing.

The desire to be transformative has its origins to a considerable extent with the TCHC, and in particular with Ballantyne. As a senior City official put it:

> It's full credit to TCHC. The City was behind on this, and the agencies around RP quite frankly were behind on this. It was really TCHC leadership and the residents who moved on this.

Another City official added that a crucial element has been "the respect that Derek [Ballantyne] has shown the residents in terms of they're an integral part of this redevelopment going forward... it's been his leadership that has really made this project successful."

Yet the residents' views are more varied. A considerable majority feel positively about the redevelopment; this was the case for all Asians who spoke with me and a majority of Black and White residents. Nevertheless, residents expressed a great deal of anxiety about relocation issues: "Will I get a new unit; are units being allocated fairly; how long will I be away from RP even if I do get a new unit?" While the TCHC insists that RP residents have a right of return and will have choices for new units, this is not fully true. Not everyone will have the choice to return to the RP footprint; some will be in one of the three off-site locations. If they want to be on the footprint — almost all of the seventy interviewees do — many will have to wait for Phase 2 to be completed, which will mean up to a five-year wait for some. And so far those residents who have returned have had to select their units from drawings. They were not allowed to see units before making their choice.

Many also expressed concerns about the impending loss of community, and a striking feature of the interviews was how very positively many RP residents feel about their community. Two Asian teenagers, for example, said they love living in RP: "It's like a family here... we know everybody." A Black man in his late teens said: "I lived here all my life. It's good. It's like a big family. Everybody knows everybody." A White mother in her early thirties observed: "Everybody looks out for everybody's kids. I think it's like, community, in every sense of the word." A White man in his fifties expressed both a common sentiment and a common concern: "Nobody really wants to leave the neighbourhood but we're all worried whether we're going to be able to get back in." This worry is rational: not everyone will get back in. The social composition of RP will change dramatically, from 100 percent of residents living in RGI units, and therefore in some sense or other being "poor," to about 70 percent of residents living in condos at market rates for downtown Toronto, and therefore almost certainly being of a different social class and not being "poor." Can the sense of community so valued by residents be maintained in this new environment?

Conflict is likely, based on experience elsewhere (Slater 2005; Smith 1996, for example). The TCHC, the City and the developer, Daniels Corporation, are aware of this and thus endlessly promote the importance of social inclusion and cohesion, and to their credit have taken steps — organizing social gatherings that include newcomers and existing tenants, for example — to bring the groups together. But already instances of condescending and even aggressive behaviour and a dramatically differing sense of community "needs" have been reported by some interviewees. And low-income people of the kind that have historically lived at RP will be dramatically outnumbered by members of the "new middle class," who seek the amenities and privileges that downtown life can offer. Indeed, a new aquatic centre and an arts and culture centre in the revitalized RP are seen as important benefits to low-income residents of RP, but they are also being used in the developer's promotional literature to attract the kinds of people who want their condos to include "a trendy glass-enclosed coffee bar that is sure to become a favourite gathering spot" and "a lounge that rivals Toronto's social hotspots, with seating areas, a sleek bar, and an outdoor terrace offering views of the city skyline" (Daniels Corporation 2010). The attempt therefore is to attract people whose definition of community is strikingly different than that valued by so many of the seventy residents I interviewed.

One long-time resident of Jamaican origin said about his community: "They're losing their culture." He and his friends can't afford $6 for a beer in a trendy bar. They have always shared funds to buy a "two-four" and then "have a few on somebody's front yard" with a bonfire going. But with the new condo owners coming in, forming a majority and imposing their will, "that will never happen again, that definitely gonna stop." It is completely valid for existing RP residents to be anxious about their future, about whether they will get a new unit at a time when low-income rental is in such short supply and, if they do, about the kind of community in which they will live.

The Role of Community-Based Organizations

Similar uncertainties are being felt by the CBOs that have historically worked in RP, most of which have emerged out of the efforts of RP tenants (TCHC 2007b: 5–17). They are being asked to change: to include higher-income newcomers among those with whom they work; to be transformative rather than ameliorative in their work. They are being told, one CBO leader said, that the goal of the redevelopment "is the creation of real avenues out of poverty, not just mitigating poverty which has really been the game in RP for the last 50 years."

Some CBOs have responded especially creatively to this challenge. The Toronto Christian Resource Centre (CRC), for example, which operates in RP with an annual budget of some $700,000, has raised $19 million to construct a new building that will include a new community hub, plus eighty-seven deeply subsidized housing units that will provide supports to those with addictions and mental illness. As with everything about the redevelopment of RP, one can interpret this in different ways. It is a remarkable achievement for a relatively small, long-time RP CBO, and the board and staff deserve full credit. Yet why is it that a $19 million investment can build eighty-seven new housing units, while a $1 billion investment, more than fifty times as much money, produces no net gain in the number of social housing units, and in fact a net loss of such units on the RP footprint? As a particularly astute community worker who grew up in RP put it to me, speaking emphatically: "Because it's not *about* creating new housing!"

There are fears and anxieties among CBOs that such catch phrases as "being transformative" and "not just mitigating poverty" may be a screen behind which to dismantle supports for residents. Given the experience with HOPE VI and thirty years of neoliberal impact on social services, such fears are rational. What is more, the transition from spatially concentrated poverty to a mixed-income community is likely, according to the leader of one CBO, to make it more difficult to attract funding. "Some of the programs in the near future won't be fundable. When you look at at-risk youth programs [for example], they're predominantly funded because we've got a 100 percent high-risk community. We won't have that in future. So it's going to make funding opportunities much more challenging." Thus, CBOs face a loss of funding, while those low-income residents with whom they work may lose supports that ensure survival. Yet CBOs are prepared to attempt to move toward a transformative strategy, as evidenced by the CRC; indeed, they have little choice given the powerful forces behind the redevelopment of RP.

The social development strategy is multi-faceted, and much of it is consistent with what we know about place-based anti-poverty efforts. Job creation is, quite appropriately, a major thrust. The unemployment rate in RP is triple the Canadian average; only about one-half of RP residents participate in the labour force; of those who do many are in low-wage, insecure, non-union jobs; and one-third of RP households are headed by single mothers, who cite lack of childcare as a barrier to employment (RPNI 2006: 6). An "employment hub" has been established, creating a single point of access, that works not only on the supply side of the labour market, preparing low-income people for work, but also on the demand side by requiring employers — including the lead developer, sub-contractors and new commercial enterprises locating in RP — to hire local people (Ballantyne 18/12/08; City of Toronto 2007). Approximately seventy full-time jobs had been created by June 2009 in construction, according to Derek Ballantyne; in April 2010 some RP residents were beginning to work in some of the commercial enterprises located on site as part of Phase 1. The structure of the labour market has been modified insofar as new sources of supply have been mandated for employers — that is, to some extent at least, they must hire locally — consistent with what we know is needed to get low-income people into the labour market (Loewen et al. 2005).

There will also be a "children and youth hub," which will include the RP daycare and additional childcare facilities — as called for by single parents in RP — along with the successful Parents for Better Beginnings and Regent Park Focus programs. There will be an "education hub" and many educational initiatives. New low-income townhouses are designed with study space for students because, as Ballantyne put it at a December 2008 news conference: "There is a need for some quiet space somewhere for learning so that you can be successful in school." Pathways to Education is a high school support program developed by the Regent Park Community Health Centre in 2001 that has produced a remarkable turnaround in high school graduation rates (Pathways to Education 2009) — "Pathways has been what has given people hope." Post-secondary institutions are offering programs on-site at RP, and an elementary school on the RP footprint is one of Toronto's designated "inner-city model schools" and has the funding to offer a plethora of creative, extracurricular programs (Rushowy 2007).

Any interpretation of these initiatives ought to reflect their contradictory character. On one hand, the social side of the redevelopment is a huge and complex undertaking that reflects a commitment to transforming RP in such a way that residents who are poor have significantly increased opportunities to improve their lives. And there is little doubt that many RP residents are responding positively to the opportunities. On the other hand, almost all of these initiatives — improved educational and childcare opportunities, the aquatic and arts and culture centres, for example — are attempts to create the kind of community that will be attractive to the new middle class, who are the intended buyers of RP condos and who will be the new majority on that locationally attractive downtown space.

Reasons to be Cautious About the Outcomes

The "Revanchist" Challenge

Incoming, more well-to-do occupants of market units may turn against low-income residents, in a version of "revanchism" (Smith 1996). In Toronto's South Parkdale, middle-class gentrifiers hoped that "unsavoury" elements would disappear and were intolerant of "people who are not like them" (Slater 2004: 321). One long-time RP community worker worries about what will happen to those most marginalized: the homeless, those with addictions and mental illness. Middle-class newcomers, with their greater skills, may effectively silence the voices of low-income residents:

Let's face it, when you're educated you have power... lots of people are coming, English is their first language, they're very educated, work in probably mainstream. They're better equipped to organize meetings.... They're going to be the majority... you know there's going to be some conflict.

Consultations in 2006 with recently arrived, middle-class homeowners in Toronto's east downtown — an analytical surrogate for those who will be moving into RP — found them unprepared to be socially inclusive if doing so might adversely affect their property values (TCHC 2007d: 18). It is known that children and their activities, in and out of school, are the best means of drawing adults together across ethnic and class lines (TCHC 2007a: 26–28). Yet most of those who have recently moved into Toronto's east downtown are singles or childless couples; market units in RP are being designed for this demographic (TCHC 2007b: 27). Social inclusion and cohesion will be difficult.

The TCHC (2007a: 12) is aware of this, observing: "Without interventions there are often divisions between groups of residents in new mixed-income communities." New community practices and new roles by CBOs are among the means by which it is hoped to promote social cohesion and inclusion, and according to a community worker much thought is being directed to this (see also TCHC 2007c; 2007d). It will, nevertheless, be a major challenge.

The Problem of Image

The struggle over RP is taking place primarily at a material level, having to do with the economic and social needs of different players in the redevelopment. The developer needs to attract middle-class newcomers to purchase condos in a previously stigmatized area in order to earn the profits that are its driving force. Most existing tenants want improved, low-income rental housing. Many also want to retain the strong sense of community that has made RP an attractive home — contrary to the stereotypes and stigma typically associated with RP. These are economic and social struggles. Yet the redevelopment of RP also involves a struggle at the level of discourse and of image. The images attached to urban spaces change over time (Whitzman 2009), and images affect economic and social realities.

RP has long been socially stigmatized as a "slum," yet interviews with RP residents make it clear that these images are partial and misleading, constructed largely by those who have had no personal experience of life in RP. Many residents see RP as their home and use terms like "community" and "one big family" to express their emotional and social attachment.

In addition to these two images — RP as "slum"; RP as "one big family" — a third image will be carefully constructed, by the developer and the TCHC, in order to sell RP to people of a different social class and different material and social and cultural interests. The new middle class want a wide range of amenities and a dynamic sense of diversity, albeit of a tightly controlled kind. They want an "urban village" (Whitzman 2009). This image can only be successfully promoted if it is largely consistent with the socio-economic reality of RP. Thus, most of the seventy residents interviewed indicated that since the redevelopment started, the neighbourhood has been safer. There is less violence, less open drug dealing. Yet one woman in her mid-twenties, who insisted that she was in a position to know, informed me that the major drug dealers have simply responded to greater policing pressure by moving to other Toronto locations to do their business. Moving illegal drug dealers to other areas, like moving poor people to other areas, may make RP look better and feel safer, but there is no net gain to society.

Newcomers and Old-Timers

There is also the challenge of ensuring that *all* tenants of RP benefit from the new opportunities. RP is not homogenous, with those who work in RP identifying a division between "newcomers" and "old-timers." Large numbers of RP residents are newcomers to Canada, arrived in recent years, "and they're excited about the redevelopment. The old-time residents are more skeptical," according to a long-time community worker.

Many recent arrivals have strong educational qualifications (City of Toronto 2007) and are described by those who work in the community as highly effective in organizing to represent their interests. They are full of hope for a better future, and the City of Toronto and local corporate interests have organized to find ways to overcome barriers to their successful entry into the labour market (Boudreau et al. 2009: 95). They and their children are most likely to benefit from new opportunities in RP.

Others have been in RP for decades and have experienced intergenerational, racialized poverty. They are more skeptical about the redevelopment, partly because, according to a community worker of Jamaican origin who grew up in RP, "they're losing a lot…. The old-timers, we call them the old-timers, right, this is more than just a place to live, this is a culture by itself for them, the RP culture." They appreciate RP for many reasons: "They don't feel isolated…, their relatives are around…, they can walk just a few blocks and see someone they know, and that's healthy." Many of these old-timers are the targets of racism, expressed in a wide variety of ways. "Clearly they're the most demonized population… racialized…. they loved that community" and now have an "overwhelming sense that they are being pushed out," said another community worker. For the adolescent children of these old-timers, there are dangers associated with relocation. They are labelled and stigmatized: "Sometimes I think there's a good chance that their life can be in danger" when relocated (for evidence of this in the case of displacement from Chicago public housing, see Hagedorn and Rauch 2007: 449–52). There are fears and anxieties among old-timers and their families, and deeply mixed feelings about the redevelopment, because RP has been home to them. Families have been raised in RP, lasting friendships have been made, struggles have been fought and gains made. One long-time community worker refers to "their sense that they kind of fought the hardest battles in the community" and that people "develop incredible bonds when in adverse conditions together." Strong people have built good lives in the midst of hardship. Many people have *chosen* to stay in RP. They feel safe there. For them, RP is not the "poster child for poverty" (Purdy 2003a: 2) that outsiders see. RP is home. Many of the old-timers who built this home place are Black women. The strength of such women, their commitment to building a better home for their families and their sense of "home" in what those from the outside label a "slum" is well known (Williams 2004; Feldman and Stall 2004). Their anxieties, fears and ambivalence about the redevelopment are well-founded.

The tension is increased, especially for the old-timers, because as one community worker put it: "The residents have kind of this distrust that they've developed over the last fifty years, the way they're treated, and the lack of maintenance, and the lack of response." Given this history, it is appropriate to be fearful that the TCHC will not fulfill its commitments. For old-timers especially, the stress associated with the redevelopment is increased not only because of a long history with housing organizations that have been unresponsive to their needs, but also because they are poor and have little power, and these are their homes and their neighbourhood that are being destroyed. There is empirical evidence to support their fears. Popkin (2006: 84–85), based on a thorough analysis of the evidence to date with HOPE VI, concludes that it is the lowest-income tenants of large inner-city public housing projects who are the least likely to benefit from their redevelopment.

Thus, the most difficult test in RP may be whether the SDP benefits the "old-timers" in RP — those who have experienced spatialized and racialized intergenerational poverty and who would benefit from the kind of long-term commitment to change that cannot now be fully guaranteed. Benefits may accrue primarily to those who have arrived in more recent years, and who have higher levels of formal education and are therefore better able to seize immediate opportunities.

The Scale and Complexity Challenge

This is a massive undertaking, a social experiment. As one community worker put it: "I mean, it's huge, it's huge… this thing that's going on that's never been done before." A senior City official concurs: "The physical redevelopment of RP is a daunting challenge to articulate and manage. The kind of community transformation, and really transformation for individuals, is an equal challenge as we're discovering." Everyone in RP feels the stress and anxiety associated with the redevelopment. "Everybody's overwhelmed," said a long-time community worker. It has to be acknowledged, she added, that "the sheer scale of that community means there's going to be no simple solutions." Large problems of necessity have emerged. Is this too large an undertaking? Is the scale of the concentrated poverty too much to tackle? Is the attempt "maybe just too utopian?"

The Challenge of Investment and Time

Will there be the political will to invest the vast sums needed, consistently and patiently over time, in order to achieve the social goals of the RP redevelopment? There are no quick fixes to spatially concentrated racialized poverty (Silver and Toews 2009). Yet already some important programs in RP are struggling for funds (RPNI 2006: 2). Fiscal austerity has long since forced tightening in most City of Toronto departments and "has had disproportionately negative effects on departments with redistributive functions" (Kipfer and Keil 2002: 236). The city's fiscal problem persists (Stanford 2008), and the consequence of decades of underinvestment in RP and other public housing projects is a capital repair deficit in the TCHC as a whole of some $200 million. "We inherited a large structural deficit," said former CEO Derek Ballantyne. If both the City of Toronto and the TCHC are financially squeezed, then who will take the lead in making the large and continuing investments that are needed to eliminate the kind of spatially concentrated racialized poverty that has characterized RP in recent decades? The TCHC (2007b: 20) has raised this question:

> Implementing the SDP, however, will require the financial and decision-making involvement of all orders of government. The City of Toronto and TCHC will not be able to implement the SDP without the cooperation and financial support of the other orders of government.

The other orders of government remain entrenched in a neoliberal philosophy opposed to large public investments in socio-economic improvement and have incurred large deficits as a result of the economic crisis that began in the fall of 2008. The likelihood, therefore, of large public investments over a long period of time directed at transforming poverty in RP is, at least with current governments, slim. A failure to invest large sums consistently over time will likely result in the persistence of spatially concentrated racialized poverty at RP.

The power to make such investments, or not, remains firmly in the hands of governments and the TCHC. The residents of RP, despite their history of resistance, have relatively little organizational power, and their mobilization will be especially difficult over the next ten years when the composition of

RP will be in a constant state of flux. There are good reasons to feel cautious about the benefits from the redevelopment of RP to the lowest-income residents.

However much anxiety the redevelopment is creating amongst some residents and CBOs, a redevelopment of RP is a necessary undertaking. Consultants Boston and Meagher (2003: 41) found that "virtually all residents saw the community in need of revitalization." My interviews with seventy residents confirmed this. Even those who are critical of many aspects of the redevelopment, including the fact — rooted in the failures of neoliberalism — that it involves the privatization of valuable public space, believe redevelopment is necessary. As described by a community worker: "Everybody knows things have to change. Redevelopment has to occur. It's not about resisting redevelopment as a concept."

It is about resisting this particular form of redevelopment. Better options were possible, options that would have contributed much more substantially to what ought to have been, but is not, the real task: housing poor people and supporting them in transforming their lives and their community in ways of their choosing.

Losing a Community: Who Benefits from Redevelopment?

The redevelopment of RP is an exceptionally large and complex undertaking, any analysis of which must be cognizant of its many complexities and contradictions. There can be little doubt that the redevelopment of RP is another instance of urban neoliberalism, intended to reclaim valuable downtown property for higher-income people. As one RP resident put it: "Fifty years ago this was not prime land; today it's prime real estate," located a mere twenty minute walk from downtown Toronto's Eaton Centre. As Jane Jacobs (quoted in Whitzman 2009: 50) described this process:

> People or uses with more money at their command, or greater respectability (in a credit society the two often go together), can fairly easily supplant those less prosperous or of less status, and commonly do so in neighbourhoods that achieve popularity.

The TCHC, the developer and the City are working hard to change the image of RP, to ensure that it achieves popularity. There is concern amongst long-term residents that in this process of image-making, the name, Regent Park, will be lost, replaced by a name with fewer negative connotations. For long-time residents, this would represent a further erosion of their sense of community.

The redevelopment is happening in the form of a public-private partnership because neoliberal governments have underinvested for decades and are not now prepared to invest the necessary large sums. The fact that $1 billion will be invested in RP without producing a net increase in low-income rental units at a time when 67,000 people in Toronto are on wait lists is a condemnation of neoliberalism and its effects, as is the fact that valuable public lands have had to be privatized to raise the necessary capital. The redevelopment of RP bears the stamp of neoliberalism, in these and other ways.

The redevelopment will benefit those residents who get new subsidized rental units, although large numbers who want new units on the footprint will be disappointed. Some who want to stay will be pushed into one of three off-site locations and thus will no longer be a part of RP; others will end up in TCHC housing elsewhere in Toronto, in some but not all cases by choice. The redevelopment will benefit residents who get jobs arising from the SDP, although the number is not likely to be large. It will benefit those who have increased access to childcare, to educational opportunities and to arts, cultural and recreational amenities, all of which are significant and commendable, although there is the risk that the character of these will shift to serve the interests of the condo owners, who will be the new majority, more than those in RGI units. The neighbourhood will look better and be safer, although it is likely that much of the crime will simply be relocated to other Toronto neighbourhoods and that at least some young men who are pushed out of RP will face increased danger. "Lots of kids can't go in certain neighbourhoods. If they do it's end of story," said a long-time RP youth worker, who was not just referring to young people involved in street gangs. Benefits to long-time RP residents will be limited; many will not benefit at all; some will be worse off than they were before the redevelopment.

Residents make clear that, contrary to popular stereotypes, many who live in RP are deeply attached to their community and see its takeover by middle-class residents — claims of the benefits of social mix notwithstanding — as being largely negative, and in some cases, for the Jamaican community for example, as initiating the loss of a valued culture. It may be said that there is a danger of romanticizing what was, in truth, a community with many negative features, and it is important to acknowledge that RP residents themselves have long struggled for some form of redevelopment of RP. Yet for many, far too many, the redevelopment will mean a loss — of a home, a neighbourhood, a community.

The anti-poverty component of the redevelopment, as embodied in the Social Development Plan, has limitations. Also, given the neoliberal ideological climate and the fiscal consequences of the economic meltdown of 2008, initiatives such as job creation and targeted training and education are unlikely to be sustained, so that the long-term and comprehensive investments that are necessary to meet the complex needs of "the truly disadvantaged" (Wilson 1987) are unlikely to happen. Those who are very poor are likely to remain very poor. Some, but by no means all, will benefit from better housing, but we know that improved housing is a necessary but not sufficient condition for the elimination of deep and complex poverty.

Chapter 5

"We're Not Goin' Nowhere"

The Case of Halifax's Uniacke Square

Uniacke Square is a 184-unit public housing project in the low-income area of North End Halifax. Located immediately north of the Halifax central business district and three short blocks from Halifax Harbour, Uniacke Square is home to the kind of spatially concentrated racialized poverty that has become common in urban areas in the past thirty years. Relative to Halifax as a whole, the proportion of residents with poverty-level incomes is high; rates of unemployment are high and of labour force participation are low; educational attainment is low; the proportion of single-parent households, particularly single-parent mothers, is high; and a high proportion of residents, approximately one-half, are of African-Canadian descent. It is a contradictory space: stigmatized by many Haligonians as a place of drugs, vice and violence; yet with a strong sense of community and enough strengths that,

The pleasant surroundings of Uniacke Square, June 2010. Photo by Jim Silver.

were a deliberate and strategic program of public investment in community-led revitalization to be undertaken — similar to what is now underway in North End Winnipeg's Lord Selkirk Park — it could become a model for healthy and vibrant, albeit low-income, communities.

Uniacke Square is threatened by the neoliberal forces shaping downtown Halifax and other urban centres and by the conditions leading to gentrification in neighbourhoods close to central business districts. These forces are putting Uniacke Square at risk of being privatized. Were this to happen, the attractive urban space where the public housing project is now located would be taken over by higher-income residents, and the housing would be lost, now and in the foreseeable future, to low-income households in need of affordable housing. It appears to be the case, however, that any attempt to privatize all or parts of Uniacke Square will meet with fierce community opposition, and that low-income, North End Halifax, where Uniacke Square is located, is in the midst of a complex process that involves more than just urban neoliberalism and gentrification. There are, to be sure, neoliberal elements to the changes gaining momentum, and some gentrification as well, but there are also significant counter-forces that may result in the creation of a genuinely mixed neighbourhood with significant numbers of low-income residents. An important part of such a positive neighbourhood redevelopment would be public investment in the form of neighbourhood revitalization that is built on the strengths of, and undertaken with and in the interests of, low-income tenants. A community-led, community-building approach is preferable for low-income people in an era when affordable, good quality, low-income rental housing is in perilously short supply. Uniacke Square could be a model for this more progressive kind of response to the problems of public housing and as such would be an important element in the broader revitalization of North End Halifax.

Remaking Halifax

Halifax is the capital of Nova Scotia and effectively the economic and cultural centre of Atlantic Canada. Built around the second largest natural ice-free port in the world, Halifax has two world-class container terminals, is a major multi-modal transport hub that is the gateway to Canada for the movement of freight from the east and is the headquarters of the east coast Navy and Coast Guard. Halifax Regional Municipality (HRM) is home to six universities and the largest and most sophisticated health facilities in the region, boasts an attractive downtown harbour-front with a well-maintained historical district, offers a natural environment in its surrounding areas that is exceptionally attractive and is a major tourist centre (HRM 2006: 83). City leaders are seeking to position Halifax for what they see as being the world of the twenty-first century, hoping to build on the strengths of the city in order to attract mobile businesses and skilled, upper-income people with purchasing power and a desire for a sophisticated urban lifestyle. Other cities, Vancouver and Toronto among them, are doing the same (Hackworth 2007). In the case of Halifax, this involves, among other measures, concentrated efforts to promote "central city revitalization" and "capital city image enhancement" and to "provide a high quality living environment, a wide range of civic and cultural amenities and a vibrant arts and entertainment scene" in order to "attract well-educated individuals who are willing to pay" for such a lifestyle (HRM April 2004: 13). Those developing this kind of urban strategy, intended to position Halifax favourably in the "war of places" (HRM April 2004: 2) being fought between cities in an increasingly competitive global environment, identify Halifax's relatively high ranking in the "talent index" and "bohemian index" as strengths upon which to build. Halifax ranks fourteenth in North America in the "talent index," which measures the proportion of the population over the age of eighteen years who hold a university degree. Halifax ranks first in this index among similarly sized cities in Canada and second (after Ottawa) among cities of any size in Canada. On the "bohemian index," which measures the proportion of the population employed in artistic and creative occupations, Halifax ranks seventh in North America and second in Canada (after Victoria) among similarly sized cities (HRM April 2004: 13–14). These characteristics, the promotion of which is based on the work of Richard Florida (2002), are seen as strengths that Halifax should build upon to create a vibrant downtown and sophisticated urban culture attractive to mobile, upper-income individuals and knowledge-based companies.

This way of thinking about Halifax and its future is consistent with what elsewhere has been called the "neoliberal city." In the neoliberal city, downtowns and urban cores once abandoned as part of the mid-century process of suburbanization are now being revitalized and reconfigured, with the result that "the inner city of many large cities is now dominated by toney neighbourhoods, commercial mega-projects, luxury condominiums, and expensive boutique retail shops" (Hackworth 2007: 99). Integral to this neoliberal spatial reconfiguration of twenty-first century urban centres is the process of gentrification, which takes place at least in part to meet the needs of the kinds of people that Halifax, and most other urban centres, seeks to attract, but which places at risk such structural legacies of mid-twentieth century Keynesianism as inner-city public housing projects (149).

The risk faced by the low-income tenants of Uniacke Square, located, as they are, immediately contiguous to downtown Halifax, is that city leaders' and planners' attempts to revitalize may include the privatization of the public housing located there. The consequences could be similar to what has happened in other urban centres, Vancouver and Toronto included: a process of gentrification that serves the interests of the more well-to-do at the expense of those who are poor and that includes the elimination of public housing. This is a particularly dangerous possibility at a time when low-income rental housing is everywhere in short supply.

The Shortage of Low-Income Rental Housing

Rental housing has been in declining supply all across Canada for years, and a shortage of low-income rental housing has plagued Halifax for decades (Stephenson 1957: 36, 46). In 2001, 44 percent of renters in the Halifax Regional Municipality paid 30 percent or more of their income on shelter, a rate "which is one of the highest in the country" (HRM March 2004: iv). The proportion of Nova Scotian households paying more than 50 percent of their income on housing is the highest in the country (Fairless 2004). The income of renters in the HRM is less than half the income of home-owners, the number of new rental units being built is low and does not meet the demand, and the demand is growing as more people choose to live close to downtown (HRM March 2004: 10–12). Provincial governments in Nova Scotia have not implemented policies or programs to adequately address this problem, and the withdrawal of the federal government from provision of social housing in 1993 has meant that "since the mid-1990s, there has been virtually no production of new housing in HRM due to a lack of funds from senior levels of government," and worse, "funds are not available to maintain existing affordable housing units," putting further pressure on the supply of low-income rental units (HRM March 2004: 40). Thus, for example, there were 961 applicants on the wait list for the 184 units at Uniacke Square as of November 30, 2007, according to the Metropolitan Regional Housing Authority. By 2009, Community Action on Homelessness (2010: 2–5) reported that only 352 "affordable, self-contained rental units have been added to HRM's affordable housing stock" in the decade since 1999; a Haligonian earning the minimum wage ($8.60 per hour) and working a forty-hour week could not afford the rent for the average bachelor suite in Halifax, let alone a one- or two-bedroom apartment. More striking still, those working full-time in such necessary occupations as cook, hairstylist or retail sales could similarly not afford the rent for an average-priced bachelor suite on the 30 percent of gross wages recommended as affordable by CMHC. Two people closely involved with housing in North End Halifax said: "There was and there is a housing crisis" and "We are in a real crisis here."

The Destruction of Public Housing

It is in the context of this shortage of low-income rental housing that tens of thousands of units of subsidized public housing have been and are being destroyed across North America, making a bad situation for low-income people still worse. The destruction of public housing is best understood as the other side of the coin that involves "central city revitalization" and "capital city image enhancement" (HRM April 2004: 13). Along with this creative process goes the destructive process of removing the public housing that does not fit with the image sought by the competitive twenty-first-century city or with the needs of the mobile, upper-income individuals for whose "sophisticated" consumption tastes urban downtowns are being revitalized and reconfigured. For those who see urban downtowns in this way, public housing is considered a relic of an outmoded past. The negative stereotyping and stigmatization to which inner-city public housing projects and their residents are constantly subjected reinforce such an interpretation. In this "war of places," Uniacke Square and its tenants are at risk.

The danger signs come not only from the experience in other U.S. and Canadian cities. They can also be discerned in the history of North End Halifax in the 1960s. The wrongs committed then, described below, in the name of urban renewal and purportedly in the interests of low-income North End residents, could occur again. On the other hand, the still vivid memory of the damage done almost half a century ago are likely to serve as a means of mobilizing residents of Uniacke Square in defence of their community should the Square, as it is called by those who live there, be threatened by neoliberal forces.

The North End and Uniacke Square

Although in the nineteenth century some of the Halifax elite located their mansions on Brunswick Street overlooking the harbour, for the most part the North End was home to the working class that laboured in the area's naval dockyards and railway and associated industries. As Erickson (2004: xiii) observed: "While most industrial capitalists lived in the South End, the vast majority of industrial workers lived in the North End" in relatively modest housing. Gottingen Street became the heart of the North End, the "People's Street," bustling with shops and a wide variety of activities — similar to North End Winnipeg's Selkirk Avenue. The 1917 Halifax Explosion levelled much of the northerly portion of the North End, and out of its destruction emerged the Hydrostone district, with its modest and attractive row houses and boulevards, located to the west of Needham Hill, where the monument to the Explosion now stands (Morton 1995). The southerly part of the North End and Africville, at the northern tip of the peninsula overlooking the Bedford Basin, were largely spared from the effects of the Explosion.

Two decades later, the Second World War created an economic boom — as times of war have always done in this naval city — experienced in the working-class North End in the form of a dramatically increased demand for housing. As Erickson (2004: xvii) describes it:

To house the necessary workforce, owners of nearby North End dwellings carved them up into flats, apartments and rooms. As a result, the housing stock, already frayed from decades of use and neglect, deteriorated even more.

From this North End neighbourhood, with its deteriorated housing stock, many thousands of residents would relocate to the suburbs in the years following the Second World War, in a process of suburbanization afoot throughout North America (Jackson 1985). Also relocated, but in their case forcibly and not to the suburbs, were the 400 African-Nova Scotian residents of Africville, located beyond the paved roads. Settled by people of African descent since at least the 1840s (Nelson 2008: 11–12), Africville was interpreted through two distinctly different lenses. The most commonly used saw Africville as a "slum," comprised of crumbling shacks without running water and modern sewage facilities, and home to various forms of sin and debauchery. The other view saw Africville, at least until the last years of its existence, as a tightly knit community centred on the Seaview African United Baptist Church, located in a near-rural setting where residents fished in and enjoyed the magnificent view of the Bedford Basin, and lived largely independent lives. To its residents, it was where they wanted to live; it was home.

In the mid-1960s, every resident of Africville was removed, some forcibly and all against their wishes. The City wanted the land on which they resided and justified their forced relocation by reference to that which was negative about Africville. The City had for decades abused the residents of Africville. In the nineteenth century they ran rail lines through the community, in some cases mere feet from existing homes. They located a "night soil" depository and the Rockhead Prison near the community, and later added the Infectious Diseases Hospital, oil storage tanks, two slaughterhouses and a tar factory. In the 1950s, an open refuse dump was located approximately 350 feet from the western-most homes. Yet by the 1960s the community still did not have running water, nor sewers, nor paved roads. "Images of badly peeling paint, outhouses, heaps of scrap metal and abandoned cars allowed Haligonians to brand Africville a shanty town or slum" (Erickson 2004: 135; see also Nelson 2008; Clairmont and Magill 1999; Stephenson 1957) and served as the justification for the forcible relocation of residents and the bulldozing of their homes. The City initially argued that they wanted the land for industrial use and the northerly extension of harbour facilities (Clairmont and Magill 1999: 137–38; Stephenson 1957: 30), and later argued, disingenuously, that the forced relocation of Africville residents was for their own good (Nelson 2008). Many moved into the newly constructed Uniacke Square, on Gottingen Street, to the south of Africville, in the heart of the North End.

A better alternative would have been possible for Africville, a conclusion that can reasonably be applied to most public housing projects today. Governments could have invested in Africville, bringing services up to the level of the rest of Halifax and building creatively on the unique strengths of the community. Residents of Africville had a strong sense of themselves as a community; few were on social assistance; most raised healthy families in their modest homes; music was an important part of the lives of many. It cannot be an exaggeration to say that racism played a powerful role in the historical under-investment in, and the ultimate bulldozing of, this unique community. It would be deeply ironic if Uniacke Square, to which many were relocated, were now to suffer a similar fate, especially when, as was the case in Africville, a better alternative is possible.

The Post-War Decline of Gottingen Street and the North End

By the time Uniacke Square was built, in 1966, in the near North End between Gottingen and Brunswick Streets, in part to house the Africville relocatees, Gottingen Street and the surrounding area were well along the

Table 5-1 Gottingen Street Indicators, 1951 to 2001

Population	1951	1961	1971	1981	1991	1996	2001
Gottingen	11,939	13,070	7584	5194	5580	4494	4943
Halifax	133,931	183,946	222,637	277,727	320,501	332,518	359,190
Gottingen as % of Halifax	8.9%	7.1%	3.4%	1.9%	1.7%	1.4%	1.3%
Persons/ Household Gottingen	4.1	4.3	3.7	2.3	2.1	1.9	2.6
% Employed Gottingen	68%	75%	58%	56%	60%	51%	46%
% Tenant-Occupied							
Gottingen	78%	76%	83%	87%	87%	87%	89.5%
Halifax	45%	45%	50%	44%	42%	40%	38%
Avgerage Household Income							
Gottingen	n/a	n/a	$6196	$13,431	$23,390	$22,389	$27,209
Halifax	n/a	n/a	$10,293	$23,807	$46,786	$48,015	$56,361
Gottingen as % of Halifax	n/a	n/a	60.2%	56.4%	50.0%	46.6%	48.3%
Incidence of Low Income							
Gottingen	n/a	n/a	n/a	58%	55%	65%	59%
Halifax	n/a	n/a	n/a	35%	34%	40%	37%

Source: Melles 2003

Table 5-2 Gottingen Street Services, 1950 to 2000

	1950	1960	1970	1980	1990	2000
Retail	95	104	69	49	36	28
Financial	2	4	3	3	1	nil
Professional	19	13	9	5	5	1
Restaurants/cafes	10	13	11	7	6	8
Entertainment	4	4	3	6	6	1
Community/social services	nil	1	4	10	13	19
Vacant buildings	1	9	9	30	25	35
Vacant lots	1	9	9	30	25	35
No return			2	11	7	16
Total retail/commercial	130	138	95	70	54	38

Source: Melles 2003: 93

path of precipitous post-war decline. The character of the decline was similar in almost all important respects to what happened in many other North American inner cities.

The deterioration of the North End Gottingen neighbourhood was dramatic. Population declined both in real terms — in 2001 it was just over 40 percent of its 1951 level — and relative to Halifax as a whole, from almost 10 percent to just over one percent. The proportion of those renting grew to just under 90 percent, compared to Halifax as a whole at less than 40 percent. The proportion of those employed dropped sharply, from approximately two-thirds in 1951 to less than half in 2001, and this is reflected in the relative drop in average household income, from 60 percent of that in Halifax in 1971 to 48 percent of Halifax in 2001, and in the growth in the proportion of those in the Gottingen area with poverty-level incomes — to 59 percent in 2001 (see Table 5.1).

Another indicator of the decline of the North End is to be found in the changing character of Gottingen Street itself. In 1950, Gottingen was the pulsing and thriving heart of the North End. Within a span of four blocks at its south end, closest to downtown, there were a total of 130 retail and commercial services. These included ten different restaurants and cafes; two movie theatres; a combined total of nineteen physicians, dentists, lawyers and tailors: "Gottingen Street was the place to shop, dine and be entertained in the city" (Melles 2003: 14). Yet over the fifty-year period to 2000, the total number of retail and commercial services located on that four-block area of Gottingen Street declined from 130 to 38, a total only slightly greater than the 35 vacancies by 2000, while the number of social and community services located there grew from one in 1960 to nineteen in 2000 (see Table 5.2).

> The abundance of social agencies, vacant buildings and vacant land evident by the year 2000 has changed the form and function of this four-block commercial district. In fact, one can no longer consider this portion of Gottingen Street a true commercial district.... The social agencies attract only service users while the under-utilized spaces discourage any [other] type of street activity — a complete transformation from its previous expression and multi-purpose utility. (Melles 2003: 93)

The Bulldozers of Urban Renewal

While a part of the explanation for the decline of Gottingen Street and the surrounding North End neighbourhood was the powerful impact that suburbanization had on inner cities almost everywhere in North America, another part was the particularly destructive "urban renewal" process of the 1960s. The area immediately south of the North End and below Citadel Hill, around Jacob Street, was bulldozed in the 1960s, and Scotia Square, a large retail/commercial/residential complex, was erected a stone's throw from the Gottingen Street entrance to the North End and attracted business away. Some of the 1600 people displaced in this process were relocated to Mulgrave Park, a large public housing project opened in 1962 and located north of Uniacke Square. Gottingen itself was re-configured from the "Main Street" of the North End to a traffic corridor designed to move cars rapidly from across the harbour in Dartmouth, over the A. Murray MacKay Bridge — one foot of which was planted where Africville had been located — to downtown and back. To achieve this, parking was banned on Gottingen, and residential buildings behind and to the east of Gottingen were bulldozed, and the 660 people who lived there relocated, to create off-street parking lots (Melles 2003: 39; see also Stephenson 1957: 25–28).

Thus, several urban renewal processes were going on at the same time in the 1960s, each having a dramatic effect on the North End. Africville was bulldozed at the North End's northernmost tip, its residents forcibly relocated to the more central and southerly areas of the North End, many to Uniacke Square, opened in 1966. At the other end, the area was similarly bulldozed, many of its residents relocated to Mulgrave Park. Thus, two of the large public housing projects now located on Gottingen Street, Mulgrave Park and Uniacke Square, were "born out of destruction of neighbourhoods" (Melles 2003: 41) that was everywhere a central and defining feature of urban renewal. As was the case elsewhere — see Chapters 4 and 6 on the Toronto and Winnipeg cases — these neighbourhoods were defined as "slums" by people in positions of authority, who viewed them from the outside, had no intimate knowledge of the lives of their residents and were unable or unwilling to see the many strengths that were there to be built upon. Different and better alternatives would have been possible.

The threat that may now be facing low-income residents of the most southerly part of the North End, and especially those residing in Uniacke Square, is the gentrification of their neighbourhood, which means the loss of their homes and removal from the area. The price of housing — home ownership and rental rates — is rising in North End Halifax, outstripping the ability of low-income people to pay. This is part of the crisis of low-income housing that prevails all across Canada. At the same time, however, recent developments may serve to counter-balance the forces of gentrification, creating a community that is *genuinely* mixed — that is, a community that is healthy and vibrant and includes significant numbers of low-income people.

Gentrification

Gentrification was first described in 1964 in the work of British sociologist Ruth Glass. Glass observed that after decades of inner-city disinvestment — the consequence in part of the post-war phenomenon of suburban sprawl — older working-class neighbourhoods in London (U.K.) were being re-settled by middle-class or higher-income groups and the original residents were being displaced.

> One by one, many of the working-class quarters of London have been invaded by the middle-classes — upper and lower. Shabby, modest mews and cottages — two rooms up and two down — have been taken over, when their leases have expired, and have become elegant, expensive residences. Larger Victorian houses, downgraded in an earlier or recent period — which were used as lodging houses or were otherwise in multiple occupation — have been upgraded once again.... Once this process of "gentrification" starts in a district it goes on rapidly until all or most of the original working-class occupiers are displaced and the whole social character of the district is changed. (Glass 1964: xviii)

All the elements of a definition of gentrification are in this passage: the movement of money into older, core area neighbourhoods, i.e., reinvestment in real estate; the movement of new and different groups of people into, and older, usually lower-income groups of people out of, such neighbourhoods;

and the resulting creation of neighbourhoods with a different social character. This process is not confined to London. "Gentrification today is ubiquitous in the central and inner cities of the advanced capitalist world" (Smith 1996: 38).

Neighbourhoods that become gentrified tend to have proximity to the central business district, or to an "elite" district, and architecturally interesting housing capable of renovation. They may have commercial facilities suitable for transformation into the kinds of shops and boutiques often associated with gentrified neighbourhoods (Beauregard 1986; Ley 1996). More broadly, gentrified neighbourhoods require "an economy that supports the production of gentrifiers," that is, an economy that produces "a substantial body of professionals and managers working for government and for universities, hospitals, and other institutions. Gentrification is limited or absent in such cities as manufacturing centres, where advanced white-collar services are weakly established" (Ley 1996: 24–25). Halifax's near North End was ripe for gentrification.

Gentrification is not inevitable in any given neighbourhood, even those "vulnerable" to the process. That this is so is in large part because gentrification is a *political* process. There are contending forces at play in any potentially gentrifiable neighbourhood. Some of those involved in the process may see the "exchange value" in a neighbourhood, that is, they see it as a place to make profits; others see the "use value" in a neighbourhood, that is, they see it as a place to live, as a community (Logan and Molotch 1987).

The result is political conflict between those who see a neighbourhood as a place to make money and those who see a neighbourhood as a place to live. The outcome of this conflict is a product of the relative strengths, skills and tenacity of the contending forces. This neighbourhood-level political conflict occurs within a broader socio-economic context: the movements of capital in search of profits; the socio-economic forces and policy decisions shaping a city's course; the shifting character of social class as the consequence of broad socio-economic change; and the role played by the state. In the process of gentrification, a neighbourhood becomes "contested space": some forces promote and some oppose gentrification (see Silver 2008).

Thus, it becomes important to identify the players contesting this space. Who sees the North End Halifax neighbourhood as "exchange value" and seeks to make profits from it? Who sees the neighbourhood as "use value" and seeks to revitalize it without displacing existing residents? In whose interests does the state act and how?

"The Condos Are Coming"

People in and around Uniacke Square believe a process of gentrification is underway in the neighbourhood. In interviews most said things like:

"property values are just going through the roof"; "gentrification is going so fast right now"; "this is a prime piece of real estate" because real estate is all about "location, location, location"; and "the condos are coming." For example, the Brickyard is a new condo development on Brunswick Street, about a block from Uniacke Square. Units started at just over $250,000 in 2007, and in 2010, a two-bedroom townhouse in the Brickyard was renting at $1400 per month, while the average rent for a two-bedroom apartment in Halifax in 2009 was $877 (CAH 2010: 2). The Brickyard features "modern amenities for a contemporary urban lifestyle" and is for "those who appreciate the convenience and verve of city living" (Domus Realty website). Located two streets down from the Brickyard, facing the harbour, is Spice, another condo development, offering "loft style condominiums in the heart of downtown" (Nova Court Properties website) and intended, as one North End community worker put it, "to get young executives to live downtown again." In May 2010, a two-bedroom unit not on the harbour side was listed at $291,000; a second condo building by the Spice developers was in the planning stages; and a condo development called Theatre Lofts, where two-bedroom units start at $269,000 and are located in "the hottest place to live in metro" (Theatre Lofts website), was in construction on Gottingen Street. Also on Gottingen is a home that in May 2007 had been flipped three times, completely gutted and listed for sale at $650,000. In North End Halifax in 2007, the average price of a detached bungalow was $160,000, and a two-storey house was $295,000. A woman who grew up in the Uniacke Square area referred to "the recent quadrupling of the price of houses on the street where she grew up" (van Berkel 2007). By May 2010, a long-time housing activist was describing North End Halifax as being "in extreme transition."

This is part of a process by which the North End neighbourhood around Uniacke Square is being consciously re-made into a part of the downtown, attractive to people with higher incomes. It is a strategy completely consistent with the objective of "central city revitalization" and "capital city image enhancement and promotion" (HRM April 2004: 13); so too are the expensive boutiques locating along Agricola Street (van Berkel 2007). All of this is part of a process of gentrification that has been underway for at least fifteen years, according to a community worker.

North End Halifax as a Mixed-Income Neighbourhood

At the same time that gentrification is at work in North End Halifax, counter-forces are developing momentum that may lead to the creation of a genuinely mixed-income community. New housing is coming on line, and some of these developments are designed to meet the financial needs of low-income people. Low-income residents who want to stay in the community may be able to do so. In that case, the redevelopment process would not really be gentrification, which displaces lower-income residents. Higher-income people would move into the North End; the area would likely look better, as "eyesore" buildings on Gottingen are removed; but there would still be many low-income people in the neighbourhood. All of this is predicated, of course, upon the maintenance, as public housing, of the 184 good-quality housing units at Uniacke Square.

Some skilled and creative individuals are using innovative strategies to produce housing options for low-income residents of the North End at the same time as commercial developers are locating condos there for higher-income people. North End Halifax already has a higher proportion of social and co-op housing than other Halifax neighbourhoods, a tribute to the hard work of the local community. For example, the Creighton-Gerrish Development Association, established in 1995, is a non-profit developer that works in partnership with four community-based, non-profit societies. Headed by Grant Wanzel of the Dalhousie University School of Architecture, Creighton-Gerrish builds low-income and affordable housing in the Uniacke Square area. Wanzel provides the group with the sophisticated technical and financial knowledge necessary to produce low-income housing. It has constructed a nineteen-unit apartment building on Gottingen Street for low-income, "hard to house" singles, which is owned and managed by the Metro Non-Profit Housing Association, and six semi-detached, subsidized "affordable" houses on Creighton Street for first-time homeowners with incomes of less than $50,000. It is also preparing to build a forty-eight-unit condominium complex on Gottingen, virtually across the street from Uniacke Square, at affordable prices — starting at $129,500 for a one-bedroom unit. The strategy makes it possible for people with a long-time connection to the Gottingen area to stay in, or return to, the neighbourhood. This is important community-building work, intended to create a "decent, affordable and pleas-ant neighbourhood for the people who live there," as opposed to a trendier, more expensive area for higher-income people who do not now live there (Wanzel 2006).

An especially significant aspect of the work of Creighton-Gerrish is how difficult it is given the severe shortage of government funding and supportive policies and programs. The amount of community effort required, relative to the number of units of social and affordable housing produced, makes it unsustainable as a model for the creation of the numbers of low-income and affordable housing units that are needed. Wanzel described the work as "naked, alone and without the [necessary] financial resources" and com-mented: "Resourceless, too few housing activists and non-profit developers find themselves fighting too many battles on too many fronts." Given this, what Creighton-Gerrish has achieved is remarkable: "Creighton-Gerrish is making a difference in the well-being of several families and many individuals." But, argues Wanzel, these gains have come as the result of "a staggering amount of effort: time and energy far beyond any reasonable estimate of what would be sustainable," with the result that the model cannot be seen as the "prototype we had hoped it would be. We can learn from it, but it's not to be emulated" (Wanzel 2006).

Nevertheless, at least one for-profit developer with a social conscience is moving into the area, perhaps inspired by Wanzel and Creighton-Gerrish. The Housing Trust of Nova Scotia, an organization set up by developer Ross Cantwell and whose board "reads like a Who's Who of the local development industry" (Bousquet 2010), purchased two properties on Gottingen in 2010 and plans to build 100-plus units on each site. A $25,000 per unit subsidy from the Canada-Nova Scotia Agreement on Affordable Housing contractually obligates the trust to set aside 115 units as "affordable" housing. Cantwell said in an interview that he believes the numbers will work out such that he can offer rental units at $225 below the market rate and that these units will be affordable for those earning $25,000–30,000 per year. His motivation is not just altruism. He argues that the lack of affordable housing in Halifax serves to drive up wages, making Halifax uncompetitive relative to other Atlantic cities in attempting to attract footloose companies and individuals.

Other developments, in various stages of production at the time of writing, will also provide housing in the area for low-income people. Plans are well underway to build an eighteen-unit supported housing complex for those now living in shelters and a shelter for women and children fleeing domestic abuse, both on Gottingen. These will be added to the six ownership units, eighteen supported housing units and forty-eight condo units by Creighton-Gerrish; the 115 affordable units by Cantwell; and, it is to be hoped, the continued presence in the area of the 184-unit Uniacke Square. These are the counter-balance to the high-priced condos of the Brickyard, Spice, the planned Spice-Two and the Lofts. This process of "extreme transition" now underway in the North End of Halifax, has led the director of Community Action on Homelessness to say, positively, that "by next year this whole street [Gottingen] will look completely different."

In whatever way this complex and dynamic process unfolds over the next decade, two conclusions can be drawn. First, governments have massively failed Canadians as regards housing. The building of low-income housing in North End Halifax will have been simply too difficult, too dependent in this case on the goodwill, creativity and hard work of highly skilled individuals, to be a viable model for the production of low-income housing. Housing is a necessity, the availability of which for all Canadians should not be left to the off chance that people with the necessary technical skills will act altruistically, expending countless hours in complex work to build housing for low-income people. As Wanzel rightly observed, this is not a sustainable model for the building of the low-income housing so desperately needed. Second, if it this difficult to create new units of social housing, then it makes good sense to defend the social housing that already exists, such as the 184 units at Uniacke Square. The loss of those 184 units would be an inexcusable waste and a shameful injustice.

Is This a Modern-Day Africville?

Uniacke Square, opened in 1966, relatively quickly took on most of the elements so typical of large, post-war, inner-city public housing projects and continues to be characterized by spatially concentrated racialized poverty. Many of those in Uniacke Square are among the *very* poor. Almost two-thirds of residents have poverty-level incomes even though labour force participation rates are relatively high; almost two-thirds are single-parent families; and almost one-half are of African-Canadian descent.

Many in Uniacke Square were caught in a cycle of poverty from the start, as the consequence not only of their being forcibly removed from Africville but also being offered few supports in their new housing at Uniacke Square. This lack of social supports — "they didn't provide nothing else but the shelter," said a long-time resident (see also Nelson 2008; Clairmont and Magill 1999) — has been typical of such urban relocation schemes in North America.

When those from Africville arrived at Uniacke Square not only was there little support, but also they faced a wall of racism and discrimination. As long ago as 1957, it was openly acknowledged: "It is only in certain parts of [North End Halifax], and not elsewhere in Halifax with the exception of Africville, that negro families can find housing accommodation" (Stephenson 1957: 32). Some residents in a neighbourhood north of Uniacke Square had already said: "We don't want Africville people here" (Clairmont and Magill 1999; see also Nelson 2008: 97). One early resident of Uniacke Square said that in the 1960s it was common for African-Nova Scotians to be told by barbers and restaurant staff, "we don't cut —— hair" and "we don't serve —— here," and he described the Halifax police force at that time as "the most racist police force in Canada"; see Nelson 2008: 56; Kimber 2006, 1992; Winks 1997: 325, 349). Remarkably, schools were not desegregated until 1955 (Melles 2003: 41), one year after the historic 1954 *Brown vs. Board of Education* ruling in the U.S. and only a decade before Uniacke Square was opened. African-Nova Scotians living in the North End were effectively denied entry into the occupations associated with the neighbouring Halifax ship and dockyards and other industries. Young Black men have long since come simply to *assume* that they will not get jobs in these places, said a long-time resident, and racism generally continues to be a defining feature of day-to-day life in and around Uniacke Square. "Racism is pronounced" in the North End; "there is racism; nothing has changed" — according to many interviewed in May 2007 (see also Melles 2003: 119–20). Striking is the extent to which racism has played a defining role in the lives of the low-income residents not only of Uniacke Square but also of Regent Park in Toronto and Lord Selkirk Park in Winnipeg.

In this context of spatially concentrated racialized poverty, it is perhaps not surprising to find violence, drugs and street sexual exploitation. The Square is known as a place where crack cocaine can be purchased; very young people — pre- or early-teens — are lured into delivering drugs; and some women, according to Constable Amy MacKay, a former community police officer in the Square, are "run by the crack... there are women who are driven by the crack." "It's a huge system," she added, fuelled by poverty and racism, and as a consequence those who live in Uniacke Square, whether caught up in this cycle or not, are stigmatized. A poll of people from across Halifax conducted in May 2010 found that 70 percent avoid certain parts of Halifax, and 49 percent of these said they avoid Gottingen Street and Uniacke Square, by far the highest avoidance rate of any area of Halifax (Boutilier 2010).

Yet repeatedly those who live and/or work in the area insist that the image of the Square is a false one. A young Black resident began our conversation with an angry denunciation of what he described as "the false negative image" of the area. Virtually every other person I spoke with insisted that the image is largely false, or at least simplistic. The reality, they argued, is more complex: people in the neighbourhood know each other; there is a strong sense of community; there are many strong families; many young people are doing well. This is not to deny that there are problems; but the problems are not as severe as the negative image would lead people from outside the community to believe, and there is more to Uniacke Square than problems. In fact, the negative image prevents outsiders from seeing the more complex, more positive, reality. The stigma and stereotypes obscure the strengths in Uniacke Square.

What is more, the stigma and stereotypes hurt the people who live there. "The stigma takes its effect," says a long-time resident. When an African-Nova Scotian goes out and about and is looked at differently or something happens, they wonder "if it's because you are Black that you're treated a certain way." Young people "wear that stigma" when they venture beyond the Square. It feeds the lack of self-esteem so common among people who are the victims of racialized poverty. "Self-esteem is a significant issue for most people" in Uniacke Square and surrounding area, says a long-time community worker. As a result, many people are reluctant to move far beyond the borders of Uniacke Square, because they know that they are looked at and judged in negative ways (Kimber 2007). It places an invisible wall — the "Berlin Wall," as one resident called it — around the Square, keeping people in. This is the case in many large inner-city public housing projects, although not at Little Mountain in Vancouver. According to Paul O'Hara, a long-time community worker at the North End Community Health Centre, it was established in 1971 a couple of blocks from Uniacke Square in part because women in the Square said they were fed up with taking their children to doctors' offices downtown or in the South End, where they were made to feel unwelcome and were looked down upon. According to a resident of the Square, when a television production crew from outside Halifax came to Uniacke Square to film an event, they were told by sources in Halifax that "you better hope that truck's got locks on it." They parked their truck elsewhere. Yet when the event and the filming were over, local residents and children pitched in to help with clean-up and the hauling and loading of equipment and were told by the television crew that they were more helpful and friendly than anyone in all the other places the crew had filmed. As was the case with Africville, the image is at odds with the much more complex, and in many important respects more positive, reality.

Yet the danger is that this negative image, the stigma and stereotypes, may serve as a justification for doing to Uniacke Square what was done to Africville a half century ago and what has been done to large inner-city public housing projects throughout North America more recently. Bennett and Reed (1999), for example, argued that in the case of Chicago's Cabrini-Green there was a deliberate strategy to construct an exaggerated and inaccurately negative image in order to justify a "redevelopment" of the project. The reason, in all such cases: others want the land. The method of removal may be different for Uniacke Square than it was for Africville, or for Little Mountain in Vancouver or Regent Park in Toronto or the massive housing projects in Chicago. There is pressure to make at least some of the units in Uniacke Square available for sale to existing tenants. Those who want this land for other purposes argue that making all or some of the units available for sale is in the interests of the residents and of the broader community: they claim that homeownership will solve many of Uniacke Square's problems. This is the argument advanced, for example, by a well-known Halifax developer who expressed the view that ownership would "give people pride." Indeed, a recent Halifax report advocated just that:

> HRM should lobby the NS Department of Community Services to consider selling at least half of the units in Uniacke Square to their current occupants, to create a critical mass of pride of ownership and community stewardship. (HRM April 2004: 11)

Yet the belief by outsiders that those in Uniacke Square do not have pride in their community is belied by the words of those who live there. One thirty-six-year-old man who has lived in Uniacke Square for twenty-six years said that it is:

> No different than if you live in the South End downtown Halifax, you know. We live in our own homes and we treat them like our own homes, you know, you can go into everybody's house in Uniacke Square and there ain't too many places you'll go and see flaws, you know, everybody treats their home like a home and we dress them up so. Like today or tomorrow you can come and walk through our homes and you'll probably think we was down the South End somewheres, you know?

But the negative image prevents outsiders from seeing this. This theme arose repeatedly in interviews with residents. A twenty-five-year resident who said, "It's like one big happy family" in the Square added: "It may not seem like that to outsiders. But if the outsiders would come in and spend a couple days and nights in our community, I think, we're friendly, hospitable.... Come into our community, find out what our community is like, don't be taking other peoples' word for what goes on in someone else's community." Yet it is almost inevitably the case that this sound advice is not taken and that public housing and its residents are judged on the basis of stigma and stereotypes rather than on personal experience.

The fear of a sale has long been a topic of conversation in and around Uniacke Square. Twenty years ago the executive director of the Black United Front of Nova Scotia warned about "the threat of another Africville-type relocation" (Clairmont and Magill 1999: xx). In 2004 the provincial Community Services minister circulated a letter to tenants assuring them that Uniacke Square would not be sold (van Berkel 2005). Yet in May 2007 the local City Councillor, Dawn Sloane, said that the fear of such a sale continues to be "the biggest issue I hear." People in Uniacke are asking: "What if they sell this place?" Kimber (2007) quotes Marcus James of the North End Public Library: "A lot of young people won't go south of the Library or north of the Square anymore. They don't feel welcome. The people here see all these $250,000 condos going up. They know that these kinds of places and low-income housing don't go together. Guess which one goes?" One resident, harking back to the destruction of Africville and linking that to the danger of losing Uniacke Square, said: "History has a way of repeating itself; this is a modern-day Africville."

It is not the bulldozer that poses the danger this time. Once units are made available for sale, commercial pressures — given the gentrification in the area — will push their prices well beyond what low-income people can afford. Once that which is public becomes private, it is subject to the powerful forces of the market, for sale at the going price, like any other commodity. If existing tenants purchase their units, they will face pressures to sell at prices that will seem to them, as people who are poor, to be a small fortune. Yet once they sell, the units will be lost forever to people of low income. Current tenants will have to leave the neighbourhood; the shortage of low-income rental units, already severe, will be made worse. "We're desperate for housing stock," said a social worker in the area, and the privatization of Uniacke Square would only deepen that desperation.

Yet, just as was the case with Africville, another solution is possible. The residents of Africville wanted to stay in their homes and their community, and wanted the City to invest in running water, modern sewage facilities and paved roads — as it had done in the rest of Halifax. The City claimed that it could not afford to do so and that the bulldozing of Africville and the forcible relocation of its residents was in the residents' own long-term interests. In the end, the amount of money spent in bulldozing Africville was roughly equivalent to what it would have taken to bring the community's services up to the level of Halifax (Nelson 2008; Kimber 2006). Not taking that option had tragic consequences, the memory of which is fresh in the minds of many in North End Halifax.

This time, residents of the Square will fight any attempt to destroy their community, by privatization or otherwise. As one resident put it: "If the alarm sounds" the community will say "we're not goin' nowhere.... They're gonna' have a huge fight.... They don't want to make that mistake again."

The Africville mistake can still be avoided in Uniacke Square. The alternative is to invest in the residents of Uniacke Square, creating opportunities and providing supports to enable them to realize those opportunities and to build their capacities and capabilities, and working with them to revitalize their neighbourhood in ways of their choosing. The result would be, in the long run, that Uniacke Square would be a healthy and pleasant neighbourhood, similar to what Little Mountain in Vancouver was, in which low-income people enjoy affordable, good quality housing in a vibrant neighbourhood characterized by the strong sense of community that already exists beneath the stigma and stereotypes.

An Alternative Way Forward for Uniacke Square

There has been substantial investment in the post-war period in the Gottingen Street area, but the neighbourhood has continued its long decline (Melles 2003). The problem, at least in part, has been that too much of the investment focused on "bricks and mortar" (Melles 2003: 88–89). But also, what social investment has been made, has not been "deliberate and strategic," says a long-time community worker, and it has not built on the strengths and involvement of the people who live there. A wide variety of social agencies have located in the area. What that community worker describes as "small clusters of opportunities" have been created. But the agencies have often in the past been unstable — they come and go, "flourish and die"; they do not work together as well as they might (Bohdanow 2006: 38); and there is no overall strategy for transformation. As another neighbourhood worker put it: "There's gotta be a bigger vision."

Some fear that the lack of vision, the absence of a strategic approach to the area, is deliberate. As one long-time neighbourhood worker put it: "The advantage to government is not to have a plan." By that he means that it may be in the interests of governments — or at least governments of a neoliberal disposition — to allow the neighbourhood to continue to deteriorate, and then blame the residents and the flaws of public housing for the problems, and use that as justification for privatizing Uniacke Square, just as Bennett and Reed (1999) argue was done to justify the "redevelopment" of Chicago's Cabrini-Green. The resulting privatization and gentrification would make the neighbourhood look better more quickly, would put the land to what some planners would call a "better and higher" use, would increase the property tax revenues of the Halifax Regional Municipality — this has been a major factor in privatization and gentrification efforts in the U.S. (Slater 2005: 54) — and would be consistent with various HRM plans, as shown earlier in this chapter. However, there is another, more difficult and necessarily more long-term path.

Building on the Assets

If an asset-based approach to community development (Kretzmann and McKnight 1993) were to be adopted at Uniacke Square, the starting point would be to identify the assets in the community and to build on them. This requires shifting from the "deficit lens" — seeing only the problems and the associated stigma and stereotypes — which is so commonly applied to Uniacke Square, to a lens that consciously identifies the community's strengths.

Perhaps the first asset in Uniacke Square is the strong sense of community that almost everyone I spoke with identified immediately. As John Fleming, senior property manager with the Metropolitan Regional Housing Authority and former property manager at Uniacke Square, and a man who grew up in poverty in the immediate area, puts it: "people know each other"; "it's a community that comes together"; there are "lots of great people" in the Square. Joan Mendes, director of the North End Parent Resource Centre, said: "Basically, there's a lot of good families in the community." Residents said such things as: "I love my community… it's like one big happy family"; "Uniacke Square is a very homey environment, I feel like it's almost, it's very family-like"; "overall I find it great, really, to live here"; "downtown, in Uniacke Square, like I say, you couldn't get a better place," and "it's a small, tight-knit community… it's definitely a sense of community here." Almost everyone said similar things: although there are problems and some are serious, nevertheless the negative image of Uniacke is overblown, or at least too one dimensional, and there are many strong people and a strong sense of community. As long-time resident and neighbourhood activist Donna Nelligan put it, in what is a good example of the strength-based approach to a community like Uniacke Square: "I look at the greatness in people before I look at the negativity."

In addition, it appears that the buildings at Uniacke Square are well maintained and in good shape. Fleming is adamant that the buildings "are in great shape," and he adds: "I'm really proud of the housing we have"; "there would be no reason for you not to want to live in them"; and "I fight for that every day." He fights for that because he believes "everyone has a right to good housing" — a radical idea given the area's, and Canada's, chronic shortage of good quality housing for the millions who are poor. The area councillor, Dawn Sloane, concurs that the buildings are "in pretty good shape," a view shared by Wanzel and Cantwell. Nelligan said: "We live in pretty nice houses. They're actually really nice compared to what's out there," and "the units are in excellent shape." Other residents felt similarly. The units constitute an especially important asset in a city in which low-income rental housing is in short supply and building new social housing is so difficult. This is an excellent basis upon which to build: the availability of solid, good quality affordable housing at a time of severe shortage of such housing; and the presence at Uniacke of some strong people and a strong sense of community.

Community-Based Organizations

There are many strong community-based organizations and social agencies working in the neighbourhood, and they do good work, even though they are generally under-funded and do not operate in as coordinated a fashion as they might — although regular meetings of service providers to overcome this problem were initiated in 2009. These include, to name just two: the North End Parent Resource Centre, which offers a range of services and supports to low-income parents, especially young Black women; and the North End Community Health Centre, "seen as the blueprint for how to run a community health clinic," according to a local community worker. The community itself stages various events: an annual Black basketball tournament that involves local youth; an annual "beautification day" that involves parents and builds community pride; and the first-ever Uniacke Square Tenants' Association Conference in 2006. Residents are actively engaged in these and other organizations and events and in some cases played the lead role in their creation. For example, a twenty-five-year resident described how a group of young moms used to meet and talk at the North End Community Health

Centre "about kids and crying and feeding time and just being isolated and we just started… talking about our problems and helping each other out and we were given a room in the back of the Health Clinic and we decided to become the 'Moms of the Square'." Other moms would "just come in and talk about their problems and being isolated and we grew and grew and we got a bigger unit up there on Gottingen Street, and we just grew right out of that, then they opened four units right here on Uniacke Street for us." Thus was created the very valuable North End Parents Resource Centre.

There is a community police office located in Uniacke Square, and the two officers operate very much in a community development fashion. Constable Amy MacKay, for example, who was stationed in Uniacke Square in 2007, visited local schools and read to children, walked around the Square and met and talked with people, voluntarily tutored two children and taught the Step-Up-to-Leadership program at George Dixon Recreation Centre. She told the story of a young boy of about eight years who she feared was at risk of heading down the wrong path. She was hesitant to speak with him for fear that he would not want to be seen speaking with the police. She finally called to him as he was walking one day to George Dixon, a few minutes away. "Can I walk with you?" she asked. He mumbled a gruff "I guess so," and they walked in silence, his eyes to the ground. When they arrived at George Dixon, the boy, dressed in baggy clothes, his hat turned sideways, unexpectedly "asked me if he could read me a book… outside where everyone can see me!" Beneath the tough exterior, beneath the image, there was an eight-year-old boy who wanted to impress an adult, and to show off his reading. The potential in such a boy is limitless; the dangers, should that potential not be nurtured, are considerable. The stigma and stereotypes through which most people and governments view public housing and its residents prevent us from seeing these realities and thus contribute to governments' consistent and tragic policy failures as regards public housing.

Women provide leadership in Uniacke Square, as is so often the case in inner-city initiatives and public housing projects (Silver 2009a, 2006a: Chapter 5). It was women in Uniacke Square who initiated the process that led to the establishment of the North End Community Health Centre and the North End Parents Resource Centre. And more recently the "PEP-Bro Divas," a group of women in Uniacke Square, emerged as leaders. According to one of their members, they called themselves the PEP-Bro Divas because they got their start with the Personally Empowering People (PEP) program and because "we felt that we were strong women in our communities and we took on the role of men"; thus Bro and Divas was included because "we're a classy group of ladies." When they had completed the PEP program the Divas wanted to use their newfound self-confidence. "So they said let's just do it," according to a community worker. They started a new incarnation of the Tenants' Association, built a skating rink in the community, were the driving forces in initiating the $70,000 redevelopment of Dixon field and organized the first-ever Uniacke Square Tenants' Association Conference in September 2006. As Constable Amy MacKay put it: "These women are strong women." They have been through hard times. They have the kinds of experiential knowledge that is invaluable and irreplaceable in doing community development work in places like Uniacke Square. They have transformed their own lives in ways that are dramatic. And it has spilled over into the community. "Older folks in the neighbourhood are noticing the change," said one of the Divas.

The Divas are an example of what is possible and of the strengths that are in Uniacke Square and can be built upon. Their work in the neighbourhood has a clear community development character. Donna Nelligan says that they believed that "if there was a change to be made [it is]... up to the residents; we want to build from within the community — up." The formation of the new Tenants' Association was a "big thing" for the Divas, says Nelligan, and she and the other women grew from the experience. In the case of the redevelopment of Dixon field, the Divas contacted the director of the George Dixon Recreation Centre and negotiated with City officials and were successful. They wanted a skating rink plus other recreational activities because "our kids were being arrested for minor things... because they had nothing to do," explained one of the Divas. The community-building character of the creation of the skating rink is revealed in a story told by Nelligan. Seniors from across Gottingen Street watched the children on the rink and got so much pleasure from it that they knit hats and scarves and gave them to the children. A connection was made across the generations. More people got involved. Everyone benefitted when the community acted together in ways of their choosing.

For the Divas, the experience has been transformational. It has been, says Nelligan, "a life-changing experience for all of us." It has included "lots of growing and learning," and the women have bonded so intensely that "we will always be a group."

The experience reveals what is possible when opportunities are made available to people to enable them to grow and when supports are there to enable them to begin to solve their own problems in ways that they determine. This is community development, and the Divas have shown the beginnings of what is possible. Much more could be done if such a method were to be linked to a deliberate and strategic approach to neighbourhood change that emerges from the people themselves and supported with public investment.

This approach has not been adopted in Uniacke Square and the surrounding Gottingen Street area to date. Money has been made available, but its effects have been limited: the investment has been too top-down, too focused on bricks and mortar, insufficiently strategic, in a fashion similar in important respects to what has happened in Winnipeg's inner city over the past fifty years (Silver and Toews 2009). It is not that investment cannot help, but rather that a particular type of public investment is needed. As Jane Jacobs (1961: 292) argued: investment is essential, "indeed it is indispensable… but it must be understood that it is not the mere availability of money, but how it is available, that is all important." There is much good work being done in the area, but the parts of it are disconnected from each other, it is mainly aimed at amelioration rather than transformation, and it is under-funded. It is not part of a deliberate and strategic approach aimed at building on the many strengths of the neighbourhood. Yet moving down such a path of neighbourhood renewal is distinctly possible, particularly if the community development principles described in the next chapter are encouraged, and if those efforts are supported by long-term public investment. This is a choice that can be made now.

Learning from Africville

Uniacke Square is at a crossroads. It sits in the middle of what has become a very valuable piece of property, located near to downtown Halifax. Gentrification is well underway in the neighbourhood, and there is a real risk that the process could swallow the Square by offering units for sale to existing tenants, thereby removing them from the financial means of low-income people in future. What is now Uniacke Square would become com-modified and then gentrified, the neighbourhood would, in some respects, look better, and governments and others would congratulate themselves for having "solved the problems." But it would, in effect, be the Africville "solution": a community would be destroyed and scattered and the people now living in Uniacke Square would be no better off, and perhaps worse. Certainly low-income people in search of good quality affordable housing in future would be worse off.

But there is an alternative, just as there was with Africville, and that is to invest in Uniacke Square and its people in a deliberate and strategic fashion, working with the residents in the community to build on the assets that are already there. This is the longer and more difficult option. But it is the only option that will benefit the low-income people who live in Uniacke Square today, and who will want to live there in future, and thus it is the only option that is morally supportable. If this were to become a part of the broader process of the revitalization of North End Halifax, which holds out the promise — not at all the guarantee — that the entire area could see an infusion of housing capital, at least some of which is aimed at meeting the housing needs of low-income people, a *genuinely* mixed community could be built that would be a model of urban redevelopment in stark and attractive contrast to the neoliberal model.

Chapter 6

Rebuilding from Within

Winnipeg's Lord Selkirk Park

Lord Selkirk Park in North End Winnipeg is different from the other public housing projects examined in this book in at least two ways. First, Lord Selkirk Park faces no gentrification pressures. It is not close to Winnipeg's central business district; the North End surrounding Lord Selkirk Park is a sprawling, low-income area, not a gentrifying area. Higher-income individuals are not looking longingly at Lord Selkirk Park and environs as a place to live, as has been the case at Little Mountain and Regent Park, and threatens to be the case at Uniacke Square. Second, Lord Selkirk Park is well into a revitalization process, described by those involved as "Rebuilding from Within," which could be a model for the redevelopment of public housing — in the interests not of the well-to-do but of those who are poor.

Aerial view of Lord Selkirk Park, taken in March or April 2010 from the seventh floor of the tower building.
Photo by Jim Silver.

Winnipeg's North End has suffered a century-long experience with deep poverty and inadequate housing. When Eastern European immigrants poured into the North End a hundred and more years ago, in such large numbers that the area came to be known as the "Foreign Quarter," developers slapped up cheaply made housing on smaller than normal-sized lots. Large profits were made. Poverty and inadequate housing have been among the characteristics of the North End ever since.

When the post-Second World War process of suburbanization led to large numbers leaving the North End for new housing and larger lots in the suburbs, the already inadequate housing stock deteriorated further. Much of it fell into the hands of absentee landlords. Housing conditions worsened. New waves of internal migrants, primarily Aboriginal people, began to arrive in Winnipeg in the 1960s and located where housing was least expensive — in the North End. Governments were reluctant to invest in public housing, or social housing of any kind, preferring to leave housing largely to the forces of the market. The housing market did not serve the North End well.

In the 1960s, after years of delay, the three levels of government finally were pushed into creating public housing, including Lord Selkirk Park, located in what had once been the heart of the Jewish North End. The Developments, as it is now called by those in the area, is a 314-unit public housing project comprised largely of two-storey townhouses, but includ-ing a single, seven-storey "tower building," originally intended for seniors. The people who first moved into the Developments were happy with their new housing, yet as was the case with public housing elsewhere, conditions gradually deteriorated and a stigma came to be attached to those who live there.

100 Years of Poverty and Bad Housing

A hundred years ago, poverty was widespread in Winnipeg's North End (Artibise 1975: 187). Houses were overcrowded, promoting unsanitary conditions and poor health. Infant mortality in the North End was 248.6 per 1000 births in 1913, compared to 116.8 in the West and South Ends. Typhoid and smallpox were concentrated in the North End: in 1904 and 1905 Winnipeg had more cases of, and more deaths from, typhoid than any city in North America (Artibise 1977: 66, 104). The strong causal connection between poverty and inadequate housing, and poor health, continues to this day in the area (Brownell et al. 2010; MacKinnon 2010; Silver 2010a). Food consumption then was inadequate, as it often is today (Fernandez and Tonn 2010), leading frequently to undernourishment. Artibise (1975: 16) describes the North End of the pre-1914 era as being characterized by "overcrowded houses and tenements, lack of sanitary installations, dirty back-yards, muddy, foul-smelling streets, and poor lighting conditions."

Then, as now, blame was placed on the moral failings of the poor. The Associated Charities Bureau wrote in 1912: "the large majority of applications for relief are caused by thriftlessness, mismanagement, unemployment due to incompetence, intemperance, immorality, desertion of the family and domestic quarrels." For this reason it was thought wrong to provide adequate levels of social assistance to those in need. Doing so, argued the Bureau, would "simply make it easier for the parents to shirk their responsibilities or lead a dissolute life" (Artibise1975: 188). The real problem, however, was inadequate wages. J.S. Woodsworth, then director of All Peoples' Mission on Stella Ave, a short walk from today's Lord Selkirk Park, conducted a study in 1913 showing that "a normal standard of living" in Winnipeg required an income of $1200, but few in the North End earned that much, and "large numbers of workmen are receiving under $600 per year, many under $500, half of what is necessary" (Artibise 1975: 187).

Winnipeg then, as now, was deeply segregated, the North End cut off from the rest of the city by the vast CPR yards and distinguished by its "foreign" character, as it is today by its Aboriginal character. As a 1912 publication put it: "For many years the North End... was practically a district apart from the city," and "those who located north of the tracks were not of a desirable character" (Artibise 1975: 160). The same views can be heard today (Silver 2010b).

Yet the North End then, as now, was home to much that was positive. Selkirk Avenue was a thriving commercial centre, filled with a dazzling variety of stores and shops, whose owners typically spoke several of the Eastern European languages used by their North End customers and made credit available when needed. In 1925, in a five-block stretch on Selkirk Avenue, there were 128 businesses, and small grocery stores could be found on most North End street corners, their owners living above or behind the store (August 2003: 9).

The area immediately around what is now Lord Selkirk Park was, early in the twentieth century, the heart of the Jewish North End, "with its own synagogues, schools, social agencies, newspapers, a complex political landscape, and a Yiddish theatre" (Blanchard 2005: 198). The streets near what are today the Developments, where currently exceptionally high rates of poverty and unemployment prevail and where two-thirds of residents are of Aboriginal descent, were inhabited by those newly arrived from Eastern Europe, especially Ukrainians, Poles and Jews, most among the working poor. Poverty was largely a working-class phenomenon:

> On Flora Avenue between King and Salter, among other people, there lived three labourers, several caretakers, two clerks, a warehouseman, and a peddler. There were also tradesmen, some with

shops on Main [Street]: a blacksmith, a printer, a tinsmith, a plumber, and a harness maker. There were three tailors.... On Stella Avenue, the street south of Flora, lived people with a similar mixture of occupations: six labourers, eight clerks, and a number of tradesmen. (Blanchard 2005: 205)

Today, far fewer residents of this neighbourhood are in the labour force. The problem a hundred years ago was low wages; the problem in Lord Selkirk Park today is still low wages, but also, for far too many residents, no wages at all and a reliance on social assistance.

A remarkably wide range of social, cultural and educational organizations were built in the North End early in the twentieth century. It is no exaggeration to describe it as a dynamic cultural centre. There were newspapers published in many European languages, churches and synagogues, music and drama societies, literary associations, sports clubs, a wide range of alternative schools which kept alive traditional cultures and languages. There were frequent public speeches, dramatic productions and musical events. A thriving co-operative sector emerged, meeting the needs of many North End residents. Labour temples were constructed, mutual aid societies created. And radical politics of a bewildering variety emerged out of the socially and culturally rich, yet economically disadvantaged, North End (Machoruk with Kardash 2000; Smith 1990; Artibise 1977).

The result was a real sense of pride in being a North Ender. As Roz Usisken (n.d.: 18) described it:

Contrary to middle class, dominant stereotypes which depicted the East European immigrant as "uncultured," as suffering from cultural deprivation, many of the North End inhabitants brought with them to the new country an extensive cultural heritage of ancient traditions... [from which] they derived a dignity denied them by the dominant society.

Then, as is the case now in the public housing projects described earlier, a strong sense of community and pride could be found beneath the stigma and stereotypes so commonly associated with poverty.

Yet much of this was unknown to those who lived in the more well-to-do parts of Winnipeg, who looked down upon residents of the North End with condescension and disdain. As a result those in positions of authority "spent only a fraction of their budgets on such community services as sanitation, health departments or welfare" (Artibise 1979: 216).

Sheltered in their lavish homes in Armstrong's Point, Fort Rouge and Wellington Crescent... the governing elite's callous stance was often the result of ignorance… for the most part they gave little serious thought to the social problems in their midst. (Artibise 1977: 54)

The inadequacy of public investment in such problems, now a central feature of neoliberalism and a major cause of spatially concentrated racialized poverty, has a long lineage in Winnipeg's North End as elsewhere.

The post-Second World War relocation of large numbers of skilled, working-age people from the North End to the suburbs and the demise of the small store commercial life centred on Selkirk Avenue took its toll on the social and cultural life of the North End, much as was the case on Gottingen Street in North End Halifax. The drama and music societies, literary associations and sports clubs, the public speeches, ethnic newspapers and radical politics, all atrophied. The North End changed dramatically.

What did not change was the housing problem, which was every bit as bad in Winnipeg as it was across Canada. A 1941 survey reported "a housing shortage of unprecedented scale." Mayor John Queen added: "Housing conditions are so bad in our city that we cannot neglect the situation any longer. There is a constant violation of health bylaws but we cannot put the people out: they have nowhere to go" (*Winnipeg Tribune*: January 28, 1942).

A 1947 fact-finding board reported to City Council that

> the provision of low-rental shelter is a chronic, country-wide problem and its solution can be achieved only on a national basis…. So far, the federal government has refused to recognize the provision of low-rental housing as a national responsibility. The municipalities, by and large, have not sufficient financial strength to meet the responsibility alone. (*Winnipeg Tribune*: July 4, 1947)

In 1949 William Courage, superintendent of Emergency Housing, told Council that "the situation is so bad that the Welfare Committee is considering placing in hotels certain families now living in garages and slum conditions"; a *Tribune* editorial opined that "housing has… now become one of society's most urgent problems" (*Winnipeg Tribune*: February 12, 1949); another editorial later that year (*Winnipeg Tribune*: September 15, 1949) observed that "it still remains true that the lower third of the housing demand has not been touched. In the past this 'lower third' has occupied overcrowded tenements or the run-down and derelict housing abandoned by the middle income group." The *Tribune* (December 17, 1949) reported that 300 families per month were applying for emergency housing, while placements averaged only thirty per month and the waitlist totaled 3000.

Slum landlords were a problem. The *Tribune* (October 14, 1959) described four who between them owned eighty-one North End dwellings and from 1955 to 1958 incurred 1497 violations of the *Health Act* — for defective walls, floors and ceilings, bed bugs, insufficient plumbing, cockroaches, insufficient heat and rats. They could not be shut down, City Council was told, because there was nowhere else to put the tenants. The "lack of low-rental housing in Winnipeg has forced people to live in houses condemned as unsanitary by the Health Department."

Yet low-rent housing was not built because the majority on Council, supported strongly by the Chamber of Commerce, opposed the subsidization of housing for those of low incomes, even while heavily subsidizing suburban sprawl (*Winnipeg Tribune*: December 29, 1959). A *Tribune* editorial of October 12, 1960, observed:

> Winnipeg's record on urban renewal and the provision of housing for low-income families borders on the disgraceful. For years there have been plans upon plans, and talk on talk. But nothing has happened. Nothing has been accomplished.

So reticent was City Council to invest in public housing that Mayor Stephen Juba told the story of being "bawled out" in Ottawa for Winnipeg's failure to get "slum clearance"/public housing projects off the ground (*Winnipeg Tribune*: May 29, 1962).

Finally, in 1960, the City identified the Salter-Jarvis area, previously the heart of the North End's Jewish quarter, the Mitzraim, as the site of Winnipeg's first urban renewal project. Parts of the area had deteriorated badly, especially Jarvis Avenue. Manley Steiman, City Health Inspector, "cites Jarvis Avenue itself as being, undoubtedly, the worst street in the entire city" (Yauk 1973: 45–46). Many houses on Jarvis had been little more than shacks from the beginning of the century; many lots, small as they were, had two or more dwellings squeezed onto them (*Winnipeg Tribune*: March 12, 1961).

Into this deteriorated housing Aboriginal people began to move when their migration to the city began in earnest in the 1960s. Many located on Jarvis and the surrounding area, where housing was cheap. Strangers to the city, unfamiliar with the complexities of urban life, they were vulnerable, as were their Eastern European predecessors decades earlier, particularly to slum landlords. "Houses became hovels and landlords fed on the ill-informed Indian and Metis people who found accommodation in the area" (Yauk 1973: 47).

Aboriginal people took over from the pre-war Jewish and other Eastern European families as new targets of racial abuse. In August 1962, the *Tribune* ran a column that began: "The police, with ponderous legal irony, call it Jarvis Boulevard. Others, with more bitterness, have named it Tomahawk Row"(*Winnipeg Tribune*: August 25, 1962). Reverend Charles Forsyth told City Council: "Whether you admit it or not, there is a tremendous race problem in Winnipeg" (*Winnipeg Tribune*: February 8, 1963).

The experience with the urban renewal process that led to the bulldozing of Salter-Jarvis and building of Lord Selkirk Park (LSP) was consistent with that elsewhere. Although one early post-war resident described Salter-Jarvis as "a good area to be poor in" (Yauk 1973: 46), and much of it could have been renovated, the entire neighbourhood was bulldozed. Most of those displaced moved into nearby residences in the private rental market where the housing was no better and often worse and where they often met with severe disapproval from existing residents. For example, in 1966, thirty residents of a neighbourhood just north of LSP told City Council that new arrivals from the bulldozed area, most of them Aboriginal, were "undesirables," adding that "the moral standards of the new residents shouldn't be tolerated anywhere" and the whole process had "just shifted the slum from the Lord Selkirk development to the Magnus Ave-McGregor St. area" (*Winnipeg Free Press*: September 27, 1966; see also Yauk 1970: 100, 151).

In the end, some 740 households were relocated from Salter-Jarvis, with only seventy — less than 10 percent — accommodated in new public housing units in one or other of Gilbert Park in northwest Winnipeg and LSP. Most who got such units were happy — rents were affordable, they were close to their old neighbourhood, and the housing was new (Yauk 1973: 135). But the housing shortage had barely been dented. In 1967 Winnipeg needed 45,000 additional units of low-income housing over the next thirty years (Metropolitan Corporation of Greater Winnipeg Planning Division 1967). Urban renewal produced approximately 500 units — about 1 percent of what was thought to be needed. To meet the estimated need would have required ninety developments the size of the 314-unit LSP and 168-unit Gilbert Park combined. In the 1960s, the City was condemning as not fit for human habitation approximately 160 houses per year, or 1600 in that decade (Silver 2006b: 21), more than three times the number of housing units created by urban renewal. When urban renewal was terminated in 1969, Winnipeg had another seven public housing projects on the drawing boards (Metropolitan Corporation of Winnipeg Planning Division 1967). They were never built; the housing crisis persisted. In 1970 there was an official wait list of 700 people for LSP; a community development worker said the real wait list was closer to 3000, because "lots of people who need its accommodation haven't bothered to apply," knowing the length of the list (*Winnipeg Tribune:* March 7, 1970). LSP was an attractive place to live, relative to what was available in the private rental market, and many wanted in.

The Decline of Lord Selkirk Park

As was the case with public housing projects throughout North America, conditions in LSP began to deteriorate in the early 1970s. The severe shortage of affordable and decent low-income rental housing in the private market pushed those facing the greatest difficulties into public housing. While initially only 25 percent of residents could be on social assistance, so that most residents in LSP were low-income working-class families, the pressure to accommodate those in greatest need forced changes. The 25 percent limit was lifted. Housekeeping requirements — in 1970 those renting in LSP could be "thrown out for bad housekeeping or causing disturbances" (*Winnipeg Tribune*: March 7, 1970) — were dropped. The "most difficult cases were put in Lord Selkirk Park," and according to Tom Yauk, former City of Winnipeg commissioner of planning, social workers would say to "troublesome" clients, by way of a threat, "how would you like to live in Lord Selkirk Park?"

The resulting concentration of poverty, and of particularly complex cases of poverty, has severely adverse effects (Wilson 1987). The problem is not public housing. The problem is that the private for-profit rental market does not come close to meeting the needs of low-income people, whose numbers — for reasons having to do with broad socio-economic forces related to neoliberalism — have grown over the past forty years. As the Developments became home to those whose lives were in greatest disarray, problems emerged. By the 1980s, life in the Developments had become so difficult that "people

Table 6-1 Poverty and Related Indicators in North End Winnipeg's Lord Selkirk Park, Relative to Winnipeg and Winnipeg's Inner City, 2006

Selected Indicator	Lord Selkirk Park	Inner City	Winnipeg
Households below Statistics Canada LICO (rate of poverty)	82.3%	39.6%	20.2%
Median household income	$15,552	$31,773	$49,790
Unemployment (15 years & over)	18.7%	7.8%	5.2%
Youth (ages 15–24) unemployment	25.0%	11.9%	11.1%
Labour force participation, 25 years & over	39.5%	64.5%	67.7%
Youth (15–24) labour force participation	37.7%	64.1%	69.5%
No certificate, diploma or degree, 15 years & over	58.7%	29.9%	23.1%
Lone-parent families, both sexes, as % of all families	60.5%	32.1%	19.5%
Aboriginal population as % of total	66.7%	21.0%	10.2%

Source: Statistics Canada, Census of Canada 2006.

just didn't want to live there anymore," said Tom Yauk. He added that by the 1990s, it was 50 percent vacant. By the mid-1990s, approximately 90 percent of residents had incomes below the low-income cut-off (LICO) and social service agencies had moved into the neighbourhood in large numbers. In 2006, conditions in Winnipeg's inner city were significantly worse than in Winnipeg as a whole, and worse still in LSP, which is clearly an example of spatially concentrated racialized poverty (see Table 6-1).

To argue that LSP, and public housing generally, is the cause of the problems associated with spatially concentrated racialized poverty is to confuse cause and effect. LSP provided affordable rental housing for those in greatest need, when the demand for such housing far outstripped the supply. With the best of intentions, the doors of LSP were opened to those with nowhere else to go. The Developments did not create these problems. Broader socio-economic forces did by producing this form of poverty in ever-increasing numbers and by organizing the production of rental housing in such a way that the supply cannot meet the demand. The Developments has been left to deal with the worst effects. As Tom Yauk put it: "Nobody dreamed that it would be 100 percent social assistance recipients." And yet something like that is what it became — home to the very poor, whose poverty was deep, complex and often intergenerational.

From the beginning, there have not been sufficient resources to deal with the complexity and scale of social problems concentrated in LSP. Governments were told before LSP was built that North End housing problems could not be solved simply by knocking down old houses and putting up new ones; their solution required a comprehensive approach with a strong social component. In June 1962, both Albert Rose, a leader in the promotion of public housing in Toronto and author of a book on Regent Park (Rose 1958), and Leonard Marsh, a pioneer in the building of Canada's social security system, were in Winnipeg and spoke to the proposed public housing project in LSP. Rose said:

> We've found that you can't just provide physical accommodation and then stop… you can't develop urban renewal and assume the people are going to settle in their new environment without giving them a tremendous amount of assisted social adjustment. (*Winnipeg Tribune*: June 7, 1962)

Marsh said the same:

> When you rebuild you must rebuild the neighbourhood and not just set up a housing project. It simply isn't enough to get rid of wretched houses. This mistake has been made again and again in Great Britain and to a certain extent in Toronto. (*Winnipeg Tribune*: June 7, 1962)

This mistake was made again in Winnipeg. Social supports were not put in place, the concentrated poverty was allowed to compound itself, and by the time the social service agencies moved into the neighbourhood in large numbers, as they had on Gottingen Street in North End Halifax and Regent Park in Toronto, their efforts were largely ameliorative and disjointed, and the poverty-related problems had had decades to reproduce themselves.

Forty Years Later: Deep Problems

People providing services in LSP offered an extraordinarily negative depiction of the community in 2005 (CCPA-Mb 2005). We were told by service providers that LSP was plagued by drugs, gangs and violence: "A lot of seniors just don't want to leave their homes. They feel vulnerable… and they feel targeted…. There's a lot of gang activity in this particular neighbourhood," and they "make life very difficult for most people who live in the area." One senior said about the neighbourhood: "Well, especially here it's drugs, that's number one…. There's more drugs in this thing here than I think half of the pharmaceutical companies in the country, especially here in the Developments, eh? There's coke [cocaine], there's crack, marijuana, everything."

A youth worker said: "In the last two years I've watched kids who were doing well with their lives just go straight down hill because they got hooked on drugs with these drug dealers. They give 'em free drugs and they're gone."

Nor was home a refuge for some of these children, the worker added:

> They have an address, but it's not a home for them, they just don't want to go home. We had some kids sleeping in vans here, 40 below, broke into a van that was parked for the winter and slept in there for three days. They just didn't want to go home, because all there is is alcohol and violence there.

Violence against women was common: domestic violence and the violence of the street sex trade. In many cases the term "street sex trade" is completely inappropriate because those involved are children, twelve or thirteen years of age and even younger. They are sexually exploited and abused (Seshia 2010). "And a lot of the really young ones are from the Dufferin-Lord Selkirk Park area," said a service provider.

Safety was, for many in the LSP neighbourhood, the number one concern. One woman said:

> Safety is a huge one. It's a huge challenge. People don't feel safe. They're afraid. They're afraid of teenagers. They're afraid of our youth. People are afraid of their own kids, they're afraid of their own partners, they're not safe in their own home.

Given this environment, people's involvement in the neighbourhood was low. When asked what was not working well, one person said: "Getting the community involved." She described it as a cycle, "with drug addiction leading to crime that becomes inter-generational, which then seems to lead to people really not being involved in their community. It seems to all be part of a very large, very unhealthy cycle for people."

People become trapped. As one community worker described it: "When you're stuck in that mode of being controlled by whatever it is, whether it's the system, or a person, or the neighbourhood, or the gangs.... When you're in it, you can't see differently," you can't see a way out, an alternative to your present circumstances. Hope is lost;, despair sets in, and change is exceptionally difficult.

> Two metaphors occur repeatedly in the comments of those inter-viewed. One is the notion of a complex web — a web of poverty, racism, drugs, gangs, violence. The other is the notion of a cycle — people caught in a cycle of inter-related problems. Both suggest the idea of people who are trapped, immobilized, unable to escape, destined to struggle with forces against which they cannot win, from which they cannot extricate themselves. The result is despair, resignation, anger, hopelessness, which then reinforce the cycle, and wrap them tighter in the web. (CCPA-Mb 2005: 24)

One person who worked in LSP in 2005, when asked what the problems in the community were then, replied:

> Poverty, poverty, poverty, and poverty are the major problems. Racism, violence against women, violence against girls. Gangs. Drug dealers. Addiction. And poverty. (CCPA-Mb 2005: 22)

When we asked people working in LSP what was working well, there were some discouraging answers:

> Right now, I don't see anything. I don't see anything at all.
> Not much seems to work. There's a lot of failures.
> I think the Developments is not working well.

Some went so far as to say:

> I would get rid of the Lord Selkirk Park as an entity.
> I'd like to just bulldoze this whole fricking place down, I hate it, I hate it, I hate what it's doing to families here. (CCPA-Mb 2005: 24, 27)

Internalized Colonization

A major part of the problem is the ongoing effects of colonization. Two-thirds of the residents of LSP are Aboriginal. Aboriginal people have long been subjected to the process of colonization, with its false assumptions about their inferiority. Many have internalized those false beliefs and carry a personal sense of shame.

This is common among oppressed people. As Metis scholar Howard Adams (1999: Introduction) puts it, many Aboriginal people "have internalized a colonized consciousness." The results are devastating, according to Michael Hart (2002: 27; see also Hart 2010):

> Once Aboriginal persons internalize the colonization processes, we feel confused and powerless.... We may implode with overwhelming feelings of sadness or explode with feelings of anger. Some try to escape this state through alcohol, drugs and/or other forms of self-abuse.

A vicious cycle is created: the assumption of Aboriginal peoples' cultural inferiority, initially advanced as a means to justify European domination, becomes internalized by Aboriginal people themselves. In response, many lash out in self-abusive ways; such behaviour then reinforces the assumptions of Aboriginal inferiority that lie at the heart of the colonial ideology. As Hart (2002: 28) describes it, the more

> Aboriginal people move further into internalizing the colonization processes, the more we degrade who we are as Aboriginal people. All of these internalized processes only serve the colonizers, who then are able to sit back and say "see, we were right." In colonizers' eyes, the usurpation is justified.

It is difficult to exaggerate the extent of the damage and pain caused to Aboriginal people as a consequence of colonization. The effects of colonization accentuate the stigma typically attached to residents of public housing projects.

Rebuilding from Within

In 2005, a revitalization effort began in LSP, coordinated by the North End Community Renewal Corporation (NECRC). Since then, important initiatives have been rolled out, and a new mood is gradually beginning to emerge amongst residents.

What is important about the Rebuilding from Within strategy is its philosophy, which has a community development character and has grown organically out of the experience of inner-city people and community-based organizations working to transform their neighbourhoods in ways identified by the people who live there. Aboriginal people have been leaders in developing and implementing this approach (Silver 2006a: Chapter 5).

This process, which has been unfolding gradually in LSP, may be a model for the revitalization of inner-city public housing projects, such as Uniacke Square in Halifax, and for other neighbourhoods characterized by spatially concentrated racialized poverty. I have been directly involved in this project, working with NECRC in a voluntary capacity since 2005.

The foundation of our work in LSP is a set of principles largely consistent with those that have emerged organically out of Winnipeg's inner city over the past thirty years and that are the product of the deep experiential knowledge of community leaders, many of whom have grown up experiencing the poverty they are now involved in combating and many of whom are Aboriginal. They have developed a way of working and thinking that is genuinely bottom-up and that is now widely spread in Winnipeg's inner city (Silver 2010c; Loxley 2007).

A first principle is to take an asset-based approach to inner-city community development (CD), as opposed to a deficit approach, which focuses on weaknesses, for example, high rates of poverty, unemployment, family dysfunction and street gang activity. These problems exist. But the starting point of change is to identify and build on strengths. In LSP we started with two major assets: the good quality, affordable housing, at a time when low-income rental housing is in very short supply; and the significant number of individuals in LSP, especially but not only women, who are strong and healthy. Since the housing units are a strength, they ought not to be bulldozed as has been done elsewhere; they ought to be maintained and their life extended to the extent possible. To its credit, the provincial government adopted this view and in 2009 directed more than $17 million of its fiscal stimulus package to renovating and thus extending the life of every unit at LSP, and did the same at other Manitoba Housing projects.

There are significant numbers of strong and healthy people, especially women, in Lord Selkirk Park (Silver 2009a). The day-to-day lives of many Aboriginal women who live there are characterized by what might be called a politics of resistance. They struggle to create safe spaces for themselves and their children in a marginalized, racialized and stigmatized space. The Developments is also contested space: street gangs control certain areas, especially at night; women push back to reclaim those spaces for their children's and families' use by day. The women both accommodate, and resist, in an ongoing struggle over space. They do so in ways that, although largely invisible to the outside observer, are similar to those engaged in by poor and racialized women around the world.

Much of the women's day-to-day resistance is confined to their households and immediate surroundings, but to at least some extent they network with each other, usually in ways related directly or indirectly to their children or grandchildren. Most say they would like to create more frequent connections with other women in the neighbourhood, in a variety of ways not traditionally seen as political. One important contribution to their networking was the establishment in early 2006 of the Lord Selkirk Park Resource Centre, a safe space where residents, especially women, can meet to talk, to develop relationships and to promote collective activities.

In the embattled space of LSP, many Aboriginal women live with dignity and courage. Their strengths, largely hidden from the view of outsiders by the stigma and stereotypes associated with LSP, constitute the basis upon which the women themselves could take the lead in rebuilding LSP. These are the strengths upon which a strategy of renewal could be built.

The second principle guiding the Rebuilding from Within strategy is that people will take advantage of opportunities if they are tailored to fit their day-to-day circumstances, if there are supports to enable them to succeed and if they are the kinds of opportunities that people themselves want. Our focus has been to create tailored educational and job opportunities, because that is what residents have said they want. Aboriginal women in LSP, most of them mothers, said that they wanted to improve their education to get out of the trap of social assistance, but money, transport and childcare were barriers (Michell and Wark 2007). We worked to bring an adult learning centre to LSP that offers the mature grade twelve diploma free of charge and is located in the heart of the Developments. Residents can walk to class, and classes are timed to enable them to take their children to and from school and then go to class. Kaakiyow Li Moond Likol, a Michif name that means All Peoples' School, opened in September 2007. At the end of its second year, in June 2009, it graduated seven adults with grade twelve diplomas and in June 2010 graduated another eleven adults. Kaakiyow has two outstanding teachers and an equally skilled outreach/support worker. The latter and one of the two teachers are Aboriginal — a proportion consistent with the two-thirds of residents who are Aboriginal. The students of Kaakiyow have told us and, on February 4, 2010, told the minister of Housing and Community Development when she visited Kaakiyow and LSP, that the school is transforming their lives (see Chapter 1 in this book; NECRC 2009).

A third principle of the strategy is to take a holistic and transformative approach to CD. By holistic we mean that there is no single solution to the problems in LSP and that many things have to be done simultaneously. By transformative we mean that the goal of our efforts is not just to be ameliorative but rather to create the tailored opportunities and supports that will enable individuals to transform their lives and their community in ways of their choosing.

A fourth principle, closely linked to the previous three, is to develop the capacities and capabilities of people in LSP, again, in ways of their choosing. The purpose of CD is not to grow the economy or to make people rich. It is to enable people to reach their own human potential, to develop their own capacities, so that they are more able to live in ways they would choose to and are capable of living were they not burdened with the poverty and racism that is a central aspect of spatially concentrated racialized poverty.

A fifth principle is to hire locally at every possible opportunity. We are creating jobs in LSP, and those jobs are filled by qualified people who, to the greatest extent possible, live in or near the Developments and are Aboriginal. It is often easier to find qualified people who live elsewhere. But much is lost if that easier path is followed. In the long run it is better to hire locally and to train people when necessary, thus contributing to more people in the community being employed, with all the many spin-off benefits that produces. We have made this a fundamental commitment.

A sixth principle, especially important in Winnipeg, with its large urban Aboriginal population, is to work in a way that is culturally based. Colonization has stolen much from Aboriginal people. In the case of far too many individuals and families, it has stolen their self-esteem and self-confidence and their hope for a better future. It is essential in doing CD in neighbourhoods like LSP to work in a way that develops a sense of pride in being Aboriginal. Aboriginal organizations in Winnipeg's inner city and especially the North End have become exceptionally sophisticated in doing this kind of work (Silver 2006a). To the extent possible we have attempted to work in a way consistent with what has been learned about Aboriginal forms of CD, while still recognizing that one-third of the residents of LSP are not Aboriginal.

A seventh principle is the need to take a long-term approach to this work. The problem of spatially concentrated racialized poverty is deep and complex and often intergenerational. It has grown in Winnipeg's inner city for decades, despite numerous anti-poverty efforts since the 1960s (Silver and Toews 2009). There is no single solution — thus the need to be holistic — nor is there any quick fix, and thus the need to be long-term. Any community-building initiative has to take a fifteen to twenty year perspective.

An eighth and final principle, and in many respects the most important and, especially in LSP, the most difficult, is to engage residents. Good CD means resident participation and leadership, but that takes time and patience. Resident engagement has been limited to date, despite significant efforts, for at least three reasons. First, most people in LSP are very poor, and the complexity of poverty is such that it is a struggle for many simply to get through the day — a fact reflected in the title of recent publication: *It Takes All Day to be Poor* (CCPA-Mb 2009). Community workers described clearly how the cycle of poverty works to inhibit community engagement. Second, the effects of colonization and ongoing racism on the self-esteem and self-confidence of many Aboriginal people makes their active participation in CD more challenging. And third, governments' long-standing practice of funding anti-poverty efforts on a short-term, project basis has meant that initiatives emerge and then disappear when funding dries up, so that residents develop a well-founded cynicism about community engagement (Silver and Toews 2009; Silver 2002). The NECRC has regularly surveyed residents door-to-door and held community gatherings; the Resource Centre, Kaakiyow and the soon-to-be-built childcare/resource centre are the direct consequence of what residents have said they want and need in the community. But as valuable as this is, it falls short of the optimum, which is a CD process decided upon and led by the residents themselves (Arnstein 1969). We are still some distance from this goal.

However, at a community gathering in LSP in late 2009 to inform and seek input from residents, ten residents approached the NECRC wanting to constitute a residents' planning group to provide more systematic guidance and direction for the revitalization efforts. That residents have come forward in this way is evidence that the gains made to date — all things that residents themselves identified — are creating a new mood of optimism. The coordinator of the Lord Selkirk Park Resource Centre, herself an Aboriginal woman who grew up in the area, is now working with this group to build their skills and capacities and promote their direct involvement in the revitalization initiatives. It is hoped that this is the beginning of a greater resident engagement in this work.

Gains in Lord Selkirk Park

The Rebuilding from Within strategy emphasizes creating opportunities, tailoring those opportunities to the particular circumstances of those living in LSP and providing supports that enable residents to take advantage of the tailored opportunities and to develop their capacities and capabilities. Gains to date have been impressive. The first step was to create the Community Advisory Committee (CAC), comprised of all government and community-based service delivery agencies in the area, which meets monthly to share information about LSP. The meetings now attract between thirty and forty people, including small but growing numbers of residents. An independent evaluation of the CAC in 2008 reported that a new and more positive mood can be seen in the Developments. Two community workers in and around LSP since 1978 and 1983 said in the past year that they have never seen a more positive mood there — and that this was at least partly attributable to the work of the CAC (CCPA-Mb 2009: 39).

In February 2006, the Lord Selkirk Park Resource Centre was created because residents said that they wanted a safe place where they could meet, a need also identified elsewhere as a priority in public housing projects (FCM and CMHC 1993). The Resource Centre is staffed by three Aboriginal women, one full-time and two part-time, and offers a drop-in service, free laundry and phone, a clothing depot, a "community cupboard," which makes food and household items available in small quantities and at cost, and crisis and employment counselling. It attracts large and growing numbers of residents: in May 2010 there were approximately 950 visits to the Resource Centre; a year previous there were about 400 per month, and 500 in a busy month. In addition, staff members at the Resource Centre do regular outreach, visiting residents in their homes, developing relationships and connecting people with community resources and opportunities. The Resource Centre is also the catalyst for many new initiatives in LSP, based on staff members' intimate knowledge of residents' needs and strengths. Yet funding for the Resource Centre is a constant problem.

The Struggle for Funding

On June 3, 2010, Janice Goodman, Carolyn Young and I met to talk about the never-ending problem of funding for the Lord Selkirk Park Resource Centre. Janice is the director of Community Development for the NECRC. Carolyn, the director of Manidoo Gi Miini Ganaan, the childcare program at R.B. Russell High School and director of the future Family Resource Centre at LSP, is also in charge of the current LSP Resource Centre. Increasingly, residents are coming to the Resource Centre for help or just to talk. Often they say something like: "My friend was here last week and you helped her. I have a problem. Can you help me?" The Resource Centre is meeting many needs. Residents surveyed in 2009 made the following kinds of unanimously positive comments: "my family needed guidance and they helped us a lot"; "you can go there anytime or if you need help with something"; "I had no money for a call and you were the only one I could depend on"; "when I first moved here I got clothes and dishes from them"; "very compassionate and very helpful and resourceful" (NECRC 2009). The Resource Centre is a safe and positive space and is at the heart of the changes underway in the Rebuilding from Within strategy.

Yet on Friday, Carolyn informed us, she had almost had a "meltdown." Our funding is running out. We have been financially supported since 2006 by a variety of funders — the provincial government's Neighbourhoods Alive!; the Winnipeg Foundation; United Way of Winnipeg; the Winnipeg Partnership Agreement; the NECRC small projects fund; the FACT (Families and Communities Together) Coalition; and others. But each of these funders, generous though they have been, provides time-limited, project-based funding that has to be applied for over and over again. And there are limits to how long project funders will support any given initiative. Community organizations are told to become "self-sustaining." For most of those doing outstanding and necessary work, including our Resource Centre, this is simply impossible. We have almost exhausted the sources available to us to continue this patchwork process. We need core funding. Yet core funding is in short supply, despite the constant expression of concern about this problem (Silver 2002).

Janice and Carolyn, like scores of other talented inner-city community workers, spend 25–50 percent of their time on such matters — applying for, accounting for and reporting on a myriad of short-term funding streams. This is time not spent doing community development. This is a financing system that is broken. Yet, as an external evaluation of the Resource Centre concluded: "Despite the inadequate provision of financial resources, the Centre continues to exercise creativity and innovation to produce results" (Reimer 2009: 75).

We invited the minister of Housing and Community Development to come again to the Developments, which she did in the company of senior government officials. We made our case as strongly as we could. "We need core funding, permanent funding," we told her. She said she understood and would look into the issue further but insisted that government finances are tight. We explained that if the Resource Centre were to close its doors because funding had dried up, the fragile sense of community engagement that is slowly and cautiously beginning to emerge would collapse. Residents would say: "I knew that would happen. It always does." And community engagement would be set back yet again. At the time of writing, we anxiously await word about funding.

Carolyn got over her meltdown. But the stress is high, and the personal financial rewards modest. People do this work largely out of personal commitment to social justice. That they achieve so much, when working with a financing system that is wholly inadequate, is a testament not only to their creativity and effectiveness, but also to what would be possible if solutions that work were to be adequately funded.

Bringing Education to the Developments

In early September 2007, Kaakiyow Li Moond Likol opened its doors, and eighteen students have so far graduated with their grade twelve diploma. Few if any of these adults, most of whom have experienced many hardships, would have obtained their diploma had Kaakiyow not been located in LSP. What is more, adult students at Kaakiyow have told us that their children are doing better in school since they started at Kaakiyow. Today, Kaakiyow is permanently funded by the Province of Manitoba and thus not subject to the impermanence that comes with project funding. Students have made it clear on numerous occasions that Kaakiyow has had a transformative effect on their lives.

Numerous other educational initiatives are underway in Lord Selkirk Park. An adult literacy program operates three half-days per week in the Resource Centre and prepares adults whose skills need upgrading for entry into Kaakiyow or into the labour force. A university-level program in Community Recreation and Active Living (CRAL), run jointly by the University of Manitoba and University of Winnipeg, started offering courses in May–June 2009 to North End Aboriginal residents. Courses are offered in the North End, another example of taking education to the people rather than trying to send the people to distant educational facilities. Students who would not otherwise have attended a post-secondary institution are doing well in the program and have the option of completing a university degree or entering the workforce. The City of Winnipeg is supporting CRAL, hoping to hire more Aboriginal people trained in sport and recreation for work in North End community centres.

In 2010, Pathways to Education Canada — the remarkably successful high school support program that started in Toronto's Regent Park in 2001 and has dramatically cut high school drop-out rates and increased high school graduation rates (drop-out rates have declined from 56 percent to 12 percent; the proportion of students going on to post-secondary education has grown from 20 percent to 80 percent) — has begun operations in Winnipeg's North End, administered by the Community Education Development Association, a long-established inner-city CBO. It was through work being done in LSP that Pathways came to Winnipeg, and based on the experience in Toronto's Regent Park (Pathways to Education website n.d.), it is likely to begin to solve the serious problem of very low high school graduation rates in the North End (Brownell et al. 2010).

Provincial funding to create a forty-seven-space childcare/resource centre in LSP was finalized in October 2009, using funds from the province's fiscal stimulus package. Sixteen of the spaces will be infant spaces — residents have said this is the greatest need. The existing Lord Selkirk Park Resource Centre, now in two units in the Developments, will be integrated into the childcare centre, creating a family resource centre that will operate as a neighbourhood "hub" — that is, the combined childcare and Resource Centre will be a place where the community will gather and it will be the heart of ongoing revitalization initiatives. More children will benefit from early childhood education, and their parents will be able to earn their grade twelve at Kaakiyow — residents identified shortage of childcare spaces as an important barrier to furthering their education (Michell and Wark 2007). And as is the case with Kaakiyow, the family resource centre will be on a permanent funding stream, via the provincial childcare program, thus avoiding the project funding treadmill.

Job Creation and Local Hiring

The overall strategy in LSP is to increase educational opportunities and create more jobs, preferably jobs in the North End. The establishment of the childcare/resource centre is expected to create about twenty-four jobs, the firm commitment is to hire locally, and local people with the appropriate credentials are already submitting resumes.

Those graduating from Kaakiyow are much more likely to be able to find employment or to pursue further education leading to employment, and those North End Aboriginal residents who are taking university-level CRAL courses are much more likely to find employment and to do so in North End community centres.

When the provincial government invested its fiscal stimulus money in renovations of public housing units, they included a commitment to hiring locally, consistent with the CD principles now so widespread in Winnipeg's inner city. About sixty residents of LSP and Gilbert Park combined, including many young people — some of whom might otherwise have earned an income in the illegal drug trade — jumped at the chance to do meaningful and useful work in their community. The same has been the case at BUILD (Building Urban Industries for Local Development), which hires young people in the North End to do energy efficiency construction work, and at OPK (Ogijiita Pimatiswin Kinamatwin), a project designed, at the request of Aboriginal street gang members, to move street gang-affiliated ex-offenders into a different way of life (Comack et al. 2009). When the right kinds of jobs are created, people are anxious to work. At a time of impending labour shortages in the skilled trades (Loewen et al. 2005), these are precisely the kinds of initiatives that are needed.

The net result of the Rebuilding from Within strategy will be that more people in LSP will be in school or in the labour force, or both; more youngsters in public housing will be succeeding in school because their parents are going to school and because they have the support of Pathways to Education and have benefitted from early childhood education; and more adults will be improving their literacy skills.

Building a Community of Opportunity and Hope

There is evidence that the Rebuilding from Within strategy is working, although progress is slow. Safety continues to be the major issue for most residents of LSP. "It's still the youth that's what all the problems are, eh?" said a senior in the summer of 2010. "If you go down to the pub at night to get a box of beer you're running the risk of never getting home with it." A twenty-seven-year-old man who has lived most of his life in LSP said he saw a stabbing behind the tower building the week before, and "that's very common around here." Most women still do not venture outdoors after dark.

"I don't go out at night — at all!" said a twenty-seven-year-old mother of four. Others said the same and expressed concerns about the safety of their children, who are regularly exposed to street gang members and various forms of bullying and violence.

At the same time, however, many told us that safety is improving. Manitoba Housing has hired safety patrols and installed lighting in areas of the Developments that were previously dark. Residents spoke positively about these initiatives. One twenty-six-year-old mother told us: "One of the best things I've noticed is they're putting up lighting. Really bright, bright lights." It is revealing, however, that such steps were just being taken in the summer of 2010. This belated response to such important problems speaks volumes about the long abandonment by the state of its most fundamental responsibilities in public housing projects. It speaks also to the fact that residents of the Developments are slowly beginning to organize and make demands. In the previous year, on many occasions, groups of residents told Manitoba Housing that safety continued to be a problem and that lighting needed fixing.

Many positive comments were also made about the role being played by the Resource Centre. One woman, who had sought the assistance of staff at the Resource Centre in her struggles with Manitoba Housing over problems in her unit, said "I have all the confidence in the world in Dianne," and Christine and Cheryl are "awesome." A twenty-eight-year-old single mother with four children told us she feels isolated but goes regularly to the Resource Centre. "I just talk to whoever's there," and this brightens her day. Visits to the Resource Centre by residents have doubled in the last year; real needs are being met.

Residents are also thrilled with the renovations to all the units in the Developments. "I think the renovations are a great idea," said a thirty-eight-year-old woman. "It's gonna' be like moving into a new home," said a long-time, fifty-two-year-old resident about to move back into her unit in July 2010. "I can hardly wait!" she told us. "The units were in dire need of repairs," but people will now be "proud to live in nice places."

People are now choosing to stay. A twenty-six-year-old mother and her partner, who has a job, could have left LSP but didn't: "I'm comfortable now in the area," she said. The rent is a big issue for them. "Like, we have four kids… we make ends meet, but if we weren't living here," she said, their rent anywhere else in the North End would double. A thirty-eight-year-old single mother said: "They're making some really positive changes right now." Two years ago she wanted to leave; now she wants to stay. "It's all gonna' be good!" said a long-time male resident about the changes underway.

LSP is changing, however slow and difficult the process may be. There is still a stigma attached to living there. "I feel kind of embarrassed when people ask me where I live," said one of the mothers. But she and her family are staying because they can afford the rent, they like the changes that are underway, and they have "put down roots." A more stable, mixed-income community is gradually being created, but it is being built from within rather than by attracting higher-income people from outside.

A key feature of the strategy is to ensure that when residents get jobs and start earning wages, those earnings are not consumed by rent increases in the rent-geared-to-income system. We have insisted repeatedly to Manitoba Housing that unless this problem is solved we will end up "exporting our successes" as people who begin to make positive changes in their lives are driven out of the Developments by rising rents. To its credit the provincial government made changes in 2010 that will enable those earning wages to continue to take advantage of affordable rents, thus enabling the building from within of a mixed-income community.

LSP cannot be turned around overnight; there will be setbacks along the way; and the amount of time, effort and skill needed to move the relatively short distance achieved to date is extraordinary. But creating the safe space and the multiple supports that the Resource Centre provides, renovating the units so that people are "proud to live in nice places" and creating the educational and employment opportunities that people have said they wanted and the supports needed to take advantage of them, is building in LSP a community of opportunity and hope.

The Need for State Involvement

The principles set out above are an integral and necessary part of any meaningful anti-poverty strategy, and residents believe gains are being made in LSP. Nevertheless, our experience to date makes it clear that the kind of spatially concentrated racialized poverty that prevails in LSP cannot be solved unless the state plays a much larger role in investing in the community and its people than has typically been the case in public housing projects. Without greater investment in building the capacities and capabilities of the residents and the community, there are strict limits to what can be achieved by the kind of place-based anti-poverty efforts being undertaken at LSP.

A defining feature of the decline of LSP and other large inner-city public housing projects in North America has been their virtual abandonment by the state. This has been the case from the beginning. Urban renewal was predicated upon the view that simply building new housing where "slums" had once existed would solve poverty-related problems. This view turned out to be simplistic, and was seen as such very early on by knowledgeable observers such as Albert Rose and Leonard Marsh. They argued in the mid-1960s, before LSP was built, that much more was necessary than simply building new housing. Yet from the beginning in LSP and most other public housing projects, little socio-economic support was provided to low-income residents, and in its absence and in the context of other broad socio-economic forces, a long process of decline set in as public housing became housing of last resort for those who are poor, marginalized and racialized. This was especially true in the U.S., where Venkatesh (2000), examining the case of Robert Taylor Homes in Chicago, describes in detail the virtual abandonment by the state of that vast housing project, while Wacquant (2008) shows clearly that large public housing projects in Paris, France, while not without difficulties, were not nearly as troubled because the French state played a more interventionist role.

The state has played what might be described as an ameliorative role in LSP. Governments provide small amounts of funding, typically in a short-term, project-based format, to community-based organizations, sufficient to provide a relatively minimal and largely disjointed presence. Such interventions have not been sufficient to prevent conditions in LSP, as in Winnipeg's inner city generally, from steadily deteriorating, albeit not to the extent that would have been the case in the absence of such funding. With the emergence of the Rebuilding from Within strategy, the provincial NDP government proved willing to listen to the LSP community as it began gradually to make its voice heard and, when pressured sufficiently, to invest in LSP. As a result, changes have begun to occur. But the investments have been in initiatives that are best seen as being the state's responsibility to begin with. Education funding, for example, is not something for which citizens should have to pound on the table; nor should citizens have to demand that governing bodies provide street lighting in areas within their jurisdiction that are dangerous. Yet that is what we have had to do. The civic government has in most important respects abandoned the inner city, while the federal government has largely absented itself from social housing and public investment generally at the lower end of the income scale for almost two decades.

The way forward in deteriorating public housing complexes is to rebuild such communities from within, in ways of the residents' choosing, as is happening now in North End Winnipeg's Lord Selkirk Park. Gains are being made. Yet the process currently underway constitutes the necessary but not sufficient condition for transforming the poverty described in this book. The state must invest in low-income public housing projects like LSP, where the victims of broad socio-economic forces — globalization, de-industrialization, colonization, racism — have been concentrated over the past thirty years. The evidence in LSP — and elsewhere in Winnipeg's inner city (MacKinnon and Stephens 2010; Silver 2006a) — suggests that if and when the state does invest, in ways that low-income communities themselves identify, positive change, however gradual, begins to appear. But the problems of spatially concentrated racialized poverty have been allowed to fester untended for so long that there are now no quick fixes. People have been damaged by, and have internalized the pain associated with, decades of poverty and colonization, racism and stigmatization. The investment in the kinds of changes that poor people themselves identify must not only be consistent with the principles set out above but must also be an ongoing process of patient public investment, measured not in years but in decades. The evidence produced to date at Lord Selkirk Park is that doing so will transform the lives and communities of people who are poor.

Chapter 7

Building Good Places to Live

The cause of the problems that have plagued public housing these past thirty years and more has not been public housing as such, nor has it been the moral failings of the poor. The cause has been the dramatic structural changes often associated with globalization and neoliberalism, and the impact these changes have had at the urban level. Chief among these impacts have been the production of spatially concentrated racialized poverty in urban centres, in large part the consequence of changes in the structure of the labour market; the concentration of the poorest of the poor in low-rent, downtown public housing projects, in large part the consequence of the constant shortage of low-cost rental accommodation; and the relative abandonment of those spaces and those people by the state.

In Canada, the role of the state in the production of housing has been minimal. Some 95 percent of housing is produced on a for-profit basis, but there are no profits to be made in creating rental housing for the poor. As a consequence, the supply of low-income rental housing does not meet the demand; hence, the housing shortage that has confronted low-income Canadians throughout the twentieth and into the twenty-first centuries. Many of those least able to afford for-profit housing have been pushed into the little public housing that exists, making it housing of last resort for the poorest of the poor. Much of that public housing has been located in downtown areas already deemed to be slums when it was built half a century ago, making public housing complexes the epitome of the outcast spaces so common in large urban centres.

The withdrawal of the increasingly neoliberal state over the past thirty years, not only from the provision of housing but also from adequate levels of social support for those at the lower end of the income scale, has meant that large numbers of very poor people, spatially concentrated in public housing complexes, have been virtually abandoned to their own devices, their public housing left gradually to deteriorate around them. In such an environment, many negative forms of behaviour have emerged, accentuated by the rise of the illegal drug trade and the related activities of increasingly violent street gangs, comprised largely of those disconnected from a rapidly changing labour market. But the behaviour has been the consequence of the material circumstances in which such people have found themselves, not the cause of those circumstances.

The easier explanation, however, has been to blame the poor. The result has been the stigmatization and stereotyping of public housing and its residents over a long period of time, a process fueled in part by the racialized character of most public housing projects. In the public imagination, public housing complexes came to be seen as outcast spaces, their residents feared and reviled.

This negative depiction of public housing and its residents made it easier to win public acquiescence to the bulldozing, starting largely in the 1990s, of those public housing developments located on potentially profitable downtown land. Deteriorating public housing complexes that were home to a myriad of social problems stood in the way of revitalized downtowns designed to attract the kinds of young professionals who were thought, in the era of urban neoliberalism, to be necessary to build attractive urban futures. Public housing complexes, remnants of an earlier economic time, had to go. The stigmatization and stereotyping associated with public housing and its residents meant that the destruction of such complexes could be justified as being in the interests of the poor themselves.

This was precisely the reasoning that, in the 1960s, led to the bulldozing of Africville. That community had been abused and abandoned by the state, and the circumstances that inevitably resulted were used as the justification for its demolition — rather than its rebuilding — and even for the disingenuous claim that the destruction of their community was in the interests of the residents themselves.

Such destruction and related justifications are not remnants of a distant past. Vancouver's Little Mountain Housing, where poor people had previously enjoyed a good quality of life despite their low incomes, has just been bulldozed. That land, a "prime location" in a beautiful neighbourhood within easy reach of downtown Vancouver, has been sold to a developer and will eventually be home to people with higher incomes. The former residents, whose voices have been eloquent in describing their happiness with and affection for their public housing complex, have been dispersed. The land is too valuable to be used for housing for the poor; it can be the source of profits. This is the logical outcome of a system that treats land and housing as commodities.

A somewhat similar process is underway at Regent Park in Toronto, where the long-term neglect of repair and maintenance by the state has made redevelopment necessary. Many low-income residents, long in favour of a redevelopment that would improve the condition of their deteriorating homes, fear that the process now underway will accrue to their detriment and to the benefit of those of higher incomes. The area will eventually look better and be safer, and the stigma associated for decades with Regent Park is likely to be removed. But it is estimated that $1 billion will be invested in the revitalization, with no net gain whatever in the numbers of subsidized housing units, in fact a loss of such units on the current site, and with large numbers of the original inhabitants who want to remain in their community being dispersed to other parts of the city. The long wait list for access to public housing will remain. Yet the City and the developer will deem the completion of the project to be a victory in the effort to "solve" the problems associated with public housing.

There Is an Alternative

Public housing, its many problems notwithstanding, does not have to be bulldozed and replaced with condos for higher-income people. There is a better way. Public housing complexes can be good places to live. They can be places where poor people transform their lives by building their capacities and capabilities in ways of their choosing. For this to happen, two conditions have to be met. First, it is necessary to implement an asset-based form of community development that is rooted in what poor people themselves choose to do to change their lives, and especially importantly, in which the poor are themselves engaged. And second, the state has to play a positive role in this process of transformation. The first requires the active support of the second; the second requires a significant shift away from the neoliberal state to a more positive state. However likely or otherwise such a shift to a more activist state may be, it is distinctly possible. The redevelopment of public housing in the interests of its low-income residents is not at all a utopian scheme, however difficult in practice it would actually be.

The principles that might guide the kind of public housing redevelopment I advocate in this book are not difficult to describe or comprehend, but they are difficult to implement. The starting point is to identify and to build on the assets or strengths that exist in all communities, including the poorest. In the case of Winnipeg's Lord Selkirk Park and Halifax's Uniacke Square, for example, these include the good quality housing units and the presence — stigma and stereotypes notwithstanding — of a reasonable number of strong and healthy individuals and families and, to a greater or lesser extent in different housing projects, a sense of community. An asset-based community development process would then work to create opportunities tailored to peoples' practical and cultural circumstances and provide the supports necessary to enable them to take advantage of the opportunities. In the case of LSP, where such a process is now underway, this has so far taken the form of the creation of a range of educational and job initiatives, because this is what people have said they want, with tailored and culturally appropriate forms of education being brought to the community and local hiring aggressively practised.

The purpose is to make it possible for people to transform their lives and to do so in ways of their choosing. Both parts are necessary: the intention must be to transform, not ameliorate, the lives of poor people; and the transformation must take a form that the people who are poor themselves choose. This process is, of necessity, long and slow, given the depth and severity of the poverty that prevails in most public housing projects and given the deeply adverse effects on people who are poor of the internalization of this increasingly racialized form of poverty.

Especially difficult is securing the engagement of the residents of public housing in such a transformative process. They are reticent to become involved for a host of reasons that are perfectly rational, and thus the process is of necessity a long-term undertaking. It might seem easier and faster to decide upon and implement change from the outside, but such anti-poverty strategies have a long record of failure. Those who are poor can only build their capacities and capabilities by actively and personally engaging in a process of transformation they have chosen. In this important way, the poor must be the authors of their own anti-poverty solutions.

Yet they cannot do so alone. It would be naïve to believe that left to their own devices, people who are as poor and as demoralized as are many of those in public housing projects could transform their lives in ways of their choosing. For this kind of transformation to occur, significant supports are essential, and these must come from governments. Public investment is needed in a wide range of tailored educational and skill-building opportunities; in job creation and local hiring initiatives; in the provision of childcare with its early childhood education and local hiring capacities; in the development of sport and recreational and artistic and cultural activities for young people. These are services to which public housing residents are as entitled as are people with higher incomes. But the provision of those services has been abandoned over the past thirty years in the outcast spaces where public housing and its residents are to be found.

If poverty and the ills it generates today are to be solved, then public investment — guided by the kinds of principles described above — will need to be increased dramatically. This is of course precisely the opposite direction to that adopted by increasingly neoliberal governments over the past three decades. Yet neoliberal ideas and forms of governance have produced the often severe problems experienced in inner-city public housing projects, and it is neoliberalism that uses those problems as the justification for bulldozing public housing in the interests of higher-income people.

The better solution is to rebuild such communities from within, in ways of residents' choosing, as is happening in North End Winnipeg's Lord Selkirk Park, and to support such grassroots efforts with an ongoing process of patient and strategic public investment, measured not in years but in decades.

If this were to happen, public housing projects like Lord Selkirk Park and Uniacke Square would be good places to live. They would be safe and healthy communities in which to raise a family. The case of Little Mountain in Vancouver provides living proof that this is possible. The kind of philosophy and strategy described here, if adequately supported by public investment over a generation, would build the capacities and capabilities of people who live in public housing projects, many of whose lives are made miserable by the burdens of spatially concentrated racialized poverty. As evidenced by the lives of people described in this book, the cause of the problems in public housing is much less the failings of public housing as such, or the failings of the people who live there — as the stereotypes and stigma would lead us to believe — than it is the failure to invest enough of our vast wealth in such a way as to make it possible for all citizens to live in dignity in housing and in communities that are adequate and healthy.

References

Adams, Howard. 1999. *Tortured People: The Politics of Colonization*. Revised edition. Penticton, BC: Theytus Books.

Adams, Ian, William Cameron, Brian Hill and Peter Penz. 1971. *The Real Poverty Report*. Edmonton: Hurtig.

Allen, Chris, Margaret Camina, Rionach Casey, Sarah Coward, and Martin Wood. 2005. *Mixed Tenure, Twenty Years On: Nothing Out of the Ordinary*. York, UK: Joseph Rowntree Foundation and the Chartered Institute of Housing.

Anderson, Elijah. 1990. *Streetwise: Race, Class and Change in an Urban Community*. Chicago and London: University of Chicago Press.

Arnstein, Sherry. 1969. "A Ladder of Citizen Participation." *American Institute of Planners Journal* 35, 4.

Artibise, Alan. 1975. *Winnipeg: A Social History of Urban Growth 1874–1914*. Montreal: McGill-Queens University Press.

_____. 1977. *Winnipeg: An Illustrated History*. Toronto: Lorimer.

_____. 1979. *Gateway City: Documents on the City of Winnipeg 1873–1913*. Winnipeg: Manitoba Record Society in association with the University of Manitoba Press.

Atkinson, Rowland. 2005. *Neighbourhoods and the Impact of Social Mix: Crime, Tenure Diversification and Assisted Mobility*. Housing and Community Research Unit/ESRC Centre for Neighbourhood Research, CNR Paper 29.

Atkinson, Rowland, and G. Bridge (eds.). 2005. *Gentrification in a Global Context: The New Urban Colonialism*. London: Routledge.

August, Martine. 2003. *A Social History of Winnipeg's North End*. Student essay. University of Winnipeg.

_____. 2008. "Social Mix and Canadian Public Housing Redevelopment: Experiences in Toronto." *Canadian Journal of Urban Research* 17, 1.

Bacher, John. 1993. *Keeping to the Marketplace: The Evolution of Canadian Housing Policy*. Montreal and Kingston: McGill-Queen's University Press.

Balakrishnan, T.R., Paul Maxim and Rozzet Jurdi. 2005. "Social Class versus Cultural Identity as Factors in the Residential Segregation of Ethnic Groups in Toronto, Montreal and Vancouver for 2001." *Canadian Studies in Population* 32, 2.

Ballantyne, Derek. 2008. "Toronto Community Housing Corporation, News Conference." December 18. Video at <http://www.vvcnetwork.ca/tch/12182008/>.

_____. 2009. "Public Housing Expectations 'Unrealistic,' Says Retiring CEO." May 4. *Toronto Community Housing Corporation News Release*.

Banfield, Edward. 1970. *The Unheavenly City*. Boston: Little, Brown.

Barnes, Trevor, Tom Hutton, David Ley and Markus Moos. 2010. "Vancouver: Restructuring Narratives in the Transnational Metropolis." In Larry Bourne, Thomas Hutton, Richard Shearmur and Jim Simmons (eds.), *Trajectories of Change in Canadian Urban Regions.* Toronto: Oxford University Press.

BC Housing. 2009. *Housing Matters BC. Putting Housing First: Progress and Achievement on British Columbia's Provincial Housing Strategy.* Victoria: BC Housing.

Beauregard, Robert A. 1986. "The Chaos and Complexity of Gentrification." In Neil Smith &and Peter Williams (eds.), *Gentrification of the City.* Boston: Allen and Unwin.

Bennett, Larry, and Adolph Reed Jr. 1999. "The New Face of Urban Renewal: The Near North Development Initiative and the Cabrini-Green Neighbourhood." In Adolph Reed Jr. (ed.), *Without Justice for All: The New Liberalism and our Retreat from Racial Equality.* Boulder, CO: Westview Press.

Bennett, Larry, Janet L. Smith and Patricia A. Wright (eds.). 2006. *Where Are Poor People to Live? Transforming Public Housing Communities.* Armonk, NY: M.E. Sharpe.

Biles, Roger. 2000. "Public Housing and the Post-War Urban Renaissance, 1949–1973." In John Bauman, Roger Biles and Kristin Szylvian (eds.), *From Tenements to the Taylor Homes: In Search of an Urban Housing Policy in Twentieth-Century America.* University Park, PA: Pennsylvania State University Press.

Birmingham, Elizabeth. 1998. "Reframing the Ruins: Pruitt-Igoe, Structural Racism, and African American Rhetoric as a Space for Cultural Critique." *International Journal of Architectural Theory* 2.

Bluestone, Barry, and B. Harrison. 1982. *The Deindustrialization of America: Plant Closings, Community Abandonment, and the Dismantling of Basic Industry.* New York: Basic Books.

Bohdanow, Stephanie. 2006. "The Gottingen Street Neighbourhood: Issues, Opportunities and Actions in Community Development." Halifax: Student research paper in author's possession.

Boudreau, Julie-Anne, Roger Keil and Douglas Young. 2009. *Changing Toronto: Governing Urban Neoliberalism.* Toronto: University of Toronto Press.

Bousquet, Tim. 2010. "Big Changes on Gottingen Street." *The Coast.* April 20.

Boutilier, Alex. 2010. "New Poll Asks HRM Residents Which Areas They Avoid for Safety Concerns." May 12. *Metronews Halifax.*

Bratt, Rachel G. 1989. *Rebuilding a Low-Income Housing Policy.* Philadelphia, PA: Temple University Press.

Brenner, Neil, and N. Theodore. 2002. "Cities and the Geographies of Actually Existing Neoliberalism." In N. Brenner and N. Theodore (eds.), *Spaces of Neoliberalism: Urban Restructuring in North America and Western Europe.* Oxford, UK: Blackwell.

Brewis, T.N. 1971. "Spatial Characteristics of the Economy." In John Harp and John R. Hofley (eds.), *Poverty in Canada.* Toronto: Prentice-Hall of Canada.

Briggs, Xavier de Souza, and Margery Austin Turner. 2006. "Assisted Housing Mobility and the Success of Low-Income Minority Families: Lessons for Policy, Practice and Future Research." *Northwestern University Journal of Law and Social Policy.* 1, 1.

Brownell, Marni, Randy Fransoo and Patricia Martens. 2010. "Social Determinants of Health and the Distribution of Health Outcomes in Manitoba." In Lynne Fernandez, Shauna MacKinnon and Jim Silver (eds.), *The Social Determinants of Health in Manitoba.* Winnipeg: Canadian Centre for Policy Alternatives-Manitoba.

Brushett, Kevin. 2001. "Blots on the Face of the City: The Politics of Slum Housing and Urban Renewal in Toronto, 1940–1970." PhD. Dissertation, Queen's University.

_____. 2007. "Where Will the People Go: Toronto's Emergency Housing Program and the Limits of Canadian Social Housing Policy, 1944–1957." *Journal of Urban History* 33, 3.

Bunting, Trudi, and Pierre Filion. 2006. *Canadian Cities in Transition: Local Through Global Perspectives.* Toronto: Oxford University Press.

Canada. 1971. *Poverty in Canada: Report of the Special Senate Committee on Poverty.* Ottawa: Minister of Supply and Services.

Canada Mortgage and Housing Corporation (CMHC). 2006. *Rental Market Report: Halifax CMA.* Ottawa: CMHC.

_____. 2009a. *Canadian Housing Observer.* Ottawa: CMHC.

_____. 2009b. *Rental Market Outlook: Vancouver and Abbotsford CMAs.* Ottawa: CMHC.

Canadian Centre for Policy Alternatives-Manitoba (CCPA-MB). 2005. *The Promise of Investment in Community-Led Renewal. The State of the Inner City Report 2005. Part Two: A View from the Neighbourhoods.* Winnipeg: CCPA-MB.

_____. 2006. *Inner-City Voices; Community-Based Solutions. State of the Inner City Report 2006.* Winnipeg: CCPA-MB.

_____. 2007. *Step-by-Step: Stories of Change in Winnipeg's Inner City. The State of the Inner City Report 2007.* Winnipeg: CCPA-MB.

_____. 2009. *It Takes All Day to be Poor: The State of the Inner City Report 2009.* Winnipeg: CCPA-MB.

Carter, Tom. 2000. *Canadian Housing Policy: Is the Glass Half Empty or Half Full?* Ottawa: Canadian Housing and Renewal Corporation.

Carter, Tom, and Chesya Polevychok. 2004. *Housing Is Good Social Policy.* Ottawa: Canadian Policy Research Network.

Chicago Commission on Race Relations. 1922. *The Negro in Chicago: A Study of Race Relations and a Race Riot.* Chicago: University of Chicago Press.

City of Toronto. 2005. *Regent Park Revitalization: Strategy for the Provision of Community Facilities.*

_____. 2007. *An Employment Plan for Regent Park: Towards a Neighbourhood of Choice and Connection.*

Clairmont, Donald, and William Magill. 1970. *Nova Scotian Blacks: An Historical and Structural Overview.* Halifax: Institute of Public Affairs, Dalhousie University.

_____. 1999. *Africville: The Life and Death of a Canadian Black Community.* Third edition. Toronto: Canadian Scholars' Press.

Coleman, Alice. 1985. *Utopia on Trial: Vision and Reality in Planned Housing.* London: Hilary Shipman.

Comack, Elizabeth, Lawrence Deane, Larry Morrissette and Jim Silver. 2009. *If You Want to Change Violence in the 'Hood, You Have to Change the 'Hood.* Winnipeg: Canadian Centre for Policy Alternatives-Manitoba.

CAH (Community Action on Homelessness). 2010. *Halifax Report Card on Homelessness 2010.* Halifax: Community Action on Homelessness.

Community Advocates for Little Mountain (CALM). 2009. *Presentation to Vancouver City Council.* April 22. Kia Salomons on behalf of CALM.

Conference Board of Canada. 2010. *Building From the Ground Up: Enhancing Affordable*

Housing in Canada. Ottawa: The Conference Board of Canada.

Copp, Terry. 1974. *The Anatomy of Poverty: The Condition of the Working Class in Montreal 1897–1929.* Toronto: McClelland and Stewart.

Cox, Oliver Cromwell. 1948. *Caste, Class and Race: A Study in Social Dynamics.* New York: Doubleday.

Crump, Jeff. 2002. "Deconcentration by Demolition: Public Housing, Poverty and Urban Policy." *Environment and Planning D: Society and Space* 20.

_____. 2003. "The End of Public Housing as We Know It: Public Housing Policy, Labor Regulation and the US City." *International Journal of Urban and Regional Research* 27, 1.

Daniels Corporation. 2010. *Onenews: The Parksider Edition.* 1, 1 (March).

Davis, Mike. 2006. *Planet of Slums.* London and New York: Verso.

Delegran, W.R. 1970. "Life in the Heights." In W.E. Mann. (ed.), *Poverty and Social Policy in Canada.* Toronto: Copp Clark.

Dennis, Michael, and Susan Fish. 1972. *Programs in Search of a Policy.* Toronto: James Lewis and Samuel.

Drake, St. Clair, and Horace R. Cayton. 1945. *Black Metropolis: A Study of Negro Life in a Northern City.* Chicago: University of Chicago Press.

Drummond, Don, Derek Burleton and Gillian Manning. 2003. *Affordable Housing in Canada: In Search of a New Paradigm.* Toronto: TD Economics Special Report.

DuBois, W.E.B. 1899 [1996]. *The Philadelphia Negro.* Philadelphia: University of Pennsylvania Press.

Eberle, Margaret, Deborah Kraus, Luba Serge, Mustel Research Group and marketPOWER Research Inc. 2009. *Results of the Pilot Study to Estimate the Size of the Hidden Homeless Population in Metro Vancouver.* Ottawa: Homeless Partnering Secretariat, Human Resources and Skills Development Canada.

Economic Council of Canada. 1968. *Fifth Annual Review.* Ottawa: Economic Council of Canada.

Engels, Friedrich. 1987. *The Condition of the Working Class in England in 1844.* New York: Penguin Books

Erickson, Paul A. 2004. *Historic North End Halifax.* Halifax: Nimbus Publishing.

_____. 2004. "Mind the Gap." *The Coast.* May 13–20.

FCM (Federation of Canadian Municipalities) and CMHC (Canada Mortgage and Housing Corporation). 1993. *Community Development, Quality of Life and Fear of Crime in Ten Public Housing Communities in Canada.* Ottawa: FCM & CMHC.

Feldman, Roberta M., and Susan Stall. 2004. *The Dignity of Resistance: Women Residents' Activism in Chicago Public Housing.* Cambridge, UK: Cambridge University Press.

Fernandez, Lynne, and Nadine Tonn. 2010. "Food Security as a Social Determinant of Health." In Lynne Fernandez, Shauna MacKinnon and Jim Silver (eds.), *The Social Determinants of Health in Manitoba.* Winnipeg: Canadian Centre for Policy Alternatives-Manitoba.

Florida, Richard. 2002. *The Rise of the Creative Class: And How It's Transforming Work, Leisure, Community and Everyday Life.* New York: Basic Books.

Fong, Eric, and Milena Gulia. 1999. "Differences in Neighbourhood Qualities Among Racial and Ethnic Groups in Canada." *Sociology Inquiry* 69, 4 (Fall).

_____. 2000. "Neighbourhood Change Within the Canadian Ethnic Mosaic,

1986–1991." *Population Research and Policy Review* 19, 2.

Fong, Eric, and Kumiko Shibuya. 2000. "The Spatial Separation of the Poor in Canadian Cities." *Demography* 37, 4.

Fraser, James C., Jonathan Lepofsky, Edward Kick and J. Patrick Williams. 2003. "The Construction of the Local and the Limits of Contemporary Community Building in the United States." *Urban Affairs Review* 38, 3.

Frazier, E. Franklin. 1932. *The Negro Family in Chicago*. Chicago: University of Chicago Press.

_____. 1939. *The Negro Family in the United States*. Chicago: University of Chicago Press.

_____. 1940. *Negro Youth at the Crossways*. Washington, DC: American Council on Education.

Fromson, Etta Elaine, Joy Kristine Hansen and Roger Madison Smith. 1959. "The Little Mountain Low-Income Housing Project: A Survey of its Welfare Aspects." Master of Social Work thesis, Vancouver: University of British Columbia,.

Fuerst, J.S. 2003. *When Public Housing Was Paradise: Building Community in Chicago*. Westport, CT: Praeger.

Galabuzi, Grace-Edward. 2006. *Canada's Economic Apartheid: The Social Exclusion of Racialized Groups in the New Century*. Toronto: New Scholars' Press.

Garner, Hugh. 1968. *Cabbagetown*. Toronto: McGraw-Hill Ryerson.

Glass, Ruth. 1964. *London: Aspects of Change*. London: Centre for Urban Studies and MacGibbon and Kee.

Goetz, Edward. 2000. "The Politics of Poverty Deconcentration and Housing Demolition." *Journal of Urban Affairs* 22, 2.

Gosselin, Emile. 1971. "The Third Solitude." In John Harp and John R. Hofley (eds.), *Poverty in Canada*. Toronto: Prentice-Hall of Canada.

Hackworth, Jason. 2005. "Progressive Activism in a Neo-Liberal Context: The Case of Efforts to Retain Public Housing in the United States." *Studies in Political Economy* 75.

_____. 2007. *The Neoliberal City: Governance, Ideology, and Development in American Urbanism*. Ithaca & London: Cornell University Press.

Hagedorn, John M. (ed.). 2007. *Gangs in the Global City: Alternatives to Traditional Criminology*. Chicago: University of Illinois Press.

_____. 2008. *A World of Gangs: Armed Young Men and Gangsta Culture*. Minneapolis and London: University of Minnesota Press.

Hagedorn, John, and Brigid Rauch. 2007. "Housing, Gangs and Homicide: What We Can Learn From Chicago." *Urban Affairs Review* 42.

Hajnel, Zoltan. 1995. "The Nature of Concentrated Urban Poverty in Canada and the United States." *Canadian Journal of Sociology* 20.

Halifax Regional Municipality (HRM). March 2004. *Municipal Land Use Policy and Housing Affordability*. Halifax: Halifax Regional Municipality.

_____. April 2004. "Public Facilities Needs and Opportunities Strategy, Final Report." Halifax: Halifax Regional Municipality.

_____. August 2006. *Regional Municipal Planning Strategy*. Halifax: Halifax Regional Municipality.

Hancock, Ange-Marie. 2004. *The Politics of Disgust: The Public Identity of the Welfare Queen*. New York & London: New York University Press.

Harding, Jim. 1971. "Canada's Indians: A Powerless Minority." In John Harp and John R. Hofley (eds.), *Poverty in Canada.* Toronto: Prentice-Hall.

Hardwick, Walter G. 1974. *Vancouver.* Vancouver: Collier-Macmillan.

Harp, John, and John R. Hofley (eds.). 1971. *Poverty in Canada.* Toronto: Prentice-Hall.

Harrington, Michael. 1962. *The Other America: Poverty in the United States.* New York: Macmillan.

Harrison, Bennett, and M. Weiss. 1998. *Workforce Development Networks: Community-Based Organizations and Regional Alliances.* Thousand Oaks, CA: Sage.

Hart, Michael. 2002. *Seeking Mino-Pimatisiwin: An Aboriginal Approach to Helping.* Halifax: Fernwood Publishing.

_____. 2010. "Colonization, Social Exclusion and Indigenous Health." In Lynne Fernandez, Shauna MacKinnon and Jim Silver (eds.), *The Social Determinants of Health in Manitoba.* Winnipeg: Canadian Centre for Policy Alternatives–Manitoba.

Hastings, Dr. Charles. 1911. *Report of the Medial Officer of Health: Dealing with the Recent Investigation of Slum Conditions in Toronto.* City of Toronto.

Hellyer, Paul. 1969. *Task Force on Housing and Urban Development.* Ottawa: Queen's Printer.

Hemmingson, Karen. 2008. "Little Mountain." Powerpoint presentation to the Planning Institute of BC. October 29.

Hirsch, Arnold. 1983. *Making the Second Ghetto: Race and Housing in Chicago.* New York: Cambridge University Press.

Hogan, James. 1996. *Scattered Site Housing: Characteristics and Consequences.* Washington, DC: U.S. Department of Housing and Urban Development.

hooks, bell. 1990. *Race, Gender and Cultural Politics.* Boston: South End Press.

Hou, Feng, and Garnett Picot. 2003. "Visible-Minority Neighbourhood Enclaves and Labour Market Outcomes of Immigrants." *Analytical Studies Branch Research Paper Series.* Ottawa: Statistics Canada.

Hulchanski, David. 2002. *Housing Policy for Tomorrow's Cities.* Ottawa: Canadian Policy Research Network.

_____. 2003. "What Factors Shape Canadian Housing Policy? The Intergovernmental Role in Canada's Housing System." Paper presented at the Conference on Municipal-Provincial Relations in Canada, School of Policy Studies, Queen's University, May 9–10.

_____. 2007. "The Three Cities Within Toronto: Income Polarization Within Toronto's Neighbourhoods, 1970–2000." Toronto: Centre for Urban and Community Studies, University of Toronto, Research Bulletin 41.

Hutton, Thomas A. 1998. *The Transformation of Canada's Pacific Metropolis: A Study of Vancouver.* Montreal: Institute for Research on Public Policy.

_____. 2008. *The New Economy of the Inner City: Restructuring, Regeneration and Dislocation in the Twenty-First-Century Metropolis.* New York: Routledge.

Jackson, K. 1985. *Crabgrass Frontier: The Suburbanization of the United States.* New York: Oxford University Press.

Jacobs, Jane. 1961. *The Death and Life of Great American Cities.* New York: Vintage Books.

_____. 1993. "Foreword." In John Sewell, *The Shape of the City: Toronto Struggles with*

Modern Planning. Toronto: University of Toronto Press.

James, Ryan. 2010. "From 'Slum Clearance' to 'Revitalization': Planning, Expertise and Moral Regulation in Toronto's Regent Park." *Planning Perspectives* 25, 1.

Jencks, Christopher. 1967. "The Moynihan Report." In Lee Rainwater and William Yancey (eds.), *The Moynihan Report and the Politics of Controversy.* Cambridge: MIT Press.

Jencks, Christopher, and Paul E. Peterson (eds.). 1991. *The Urban Underclass.* Washington, DC: Brookings Institute.

Jones, Jacqueline. 1992. *The Dispossessed: America's Underclasses from the Civil War to the Present.* New York: Basic Books.

_____. 1993. "Southern Diaspora: Origins of the Northern 'Underclass'." In Michael B. Katz (ed.), 1993. *The Underclass Debate: Views from History.* Princeton: Princeton University Press.

Joseph, Mark L., Robert J. Chaskin and Henry S. Webber. 2007. "The Theoretical Basis for Addressing Poverty Through Mixed-Income Development." *Urban Affairs Review* 42, 3.

Katz, Michael B. 1989. *The Undeserving Poor: From the War on Poverty to the War on Welfare.* New York: Pantheon Books.

_____ (ed.). 1993. *The Underclass Debate: Views from History.* Princeton: Princeton University Press.

Kazemipur, Abdolmohammad, and Shiva S. Halli. 2000. *The New Poverty in Canada: Ethnic Groups and Ghetto Neighbourhoods.* Toronto: Thompson Educational Publishing.

Kent, Tom. 2002. "For Affordable Housing: Have Ottawa Pay the Rent." *Policy Options* March.

Khosla, P. 2003. *If Low Income Women of Colour Mattered in Toronto: Breaking Isolation, Getting Involved.* Toronto: Community Social Planning Council.

Kimber, Stephen. 1992. "Taking Back the Neighbourhood." *Canadian Geographic* July/August.

_____. 2006. *Reparations.* Toronto: Harper Collins.

_____. 2007. "Inside the Square." *The Coast* March 1.

Kipfer, Stefan, and Roger Keil. 2002. "Toronto Inc? Planning the Competitive City in the New Toronto." *Antipode* 34. 2.

Klein, Seth, Marjorie Griffin Cohen, T. Garner, Iglika Ivanova, Marc Lee, Bruce Wallace and Margot Young. 2008. *A Poverty Reduction Plan for BC.* Vancouver: Canadian Centre for Policy Alternatives–BC.

Kleinhaus, Reinout. 2004. "Social Implications of Housing Diversification in Urban Renewal: A Review of Recent Literature." *Journal of Housing and the Built Environment* 19.

Kosny, Mitchell. 2005. "Unlocking the Value in Toronto's East Downtown: The Revitalization of Regent Park." Speech to the Economic Club of Toronto. March 8.

_____. 2008. "Toronto Community Housing's Submission to the 2008 Ontario Pre-Budget Consultations." January 21. <http://www.torontohousing.ca/key_initiatives/strong_foundations_strong_futures/2008_ontario_pre_budget_submission>.

Kotlowitz, Alex. 1991. *There Are No Children Here: The Story of Two Boys Growing Up In the Other America*. New York: Anchor Books.

Kretzmann, John P., and John L. McKnight. 1993. *Building Communities From the Inside Out: A Path Toward Finding and Mobilizing a Community's Assets*. Evanston, IL: Asset Based Community Development Institute, Institute for Policy Research.

Layton, Jack. 2000. *Homelessness: The Making and Unmaking of a Crisis*. Toronto: Penguin.

Le Goff, Philippe. 2002. *The Shortage of Rental Housing in Canada*. Ottawa: Parliamentary Research Branch, PRB 02-16E.

Lederer, K.M. 1972. *The Nature of Poverty: An Interpretive Review of Poverty Studies, with Special Reference to Canada*. Alberta: Human Resources Research Council.

Lee, Kevin. 2000. *Urban Poverty in Canada: A Statistical Profile*. Ottawa: Canadian Council on Social Development.

Leitner, Helga, Jamie Peck and Eric S. Sheppard (eds.). 2007. *Contesting Neoliberalism: Urban Frontiers*. New York and London: Guildford Press.

Lemann, Nicholas. 1991. *The Promised Land: The Great Black Migration and How it Changed America*. New York: Knopf.

Lewis, Oscar. 1961. *The Children of Sanchez*. New York: Random House.

_____. 1969. "The Culture of Poverty." In Daniel Patrick Moynihan (ed.), *On Understanding Poverty*. New York: Basic Books.

Ley, David. 1987. "Styles of the Times: Liberal and Neo-Conservative Landscapes in Inner Vancouver, 1968–86." *Journal of Historical Geography* 13, 1.

_____. 1996. "The New Middle Class in Central Canadian Cities." In Jon Caulfield and Linda Peake (eds.), *City Lives and City Forms: Critical Research and Canadian Urbanism*. Toronto: University of Toronto Press.

_____. 2010. *Millionaire Migrants: Trans-Pacific Life Lines*. Oxford: Blackwell-Wiley.

Ley, David, and Heather Smith. 1997. "Immigration and Poverty in Canadian Cities, 1971–1991." *Canadian Journal of Regional Science* 20, 1–2.

Lithwick, N.H. 1971. *Research Monograph 1: Urban Poverty*. Ottawa: Central Mortgage and Housing Corporation.

Loewen, Garry, Jim Silver, Martine August, Patrick Bruning, Michael MacKenzie and Shauna Meyerson. 2005. *Moving Low-Income People Into Good Jobs: Evidence on What Works Best*. Winnipeg: Canadian Centre for Policy Alternatives–Manitoba.

Logan, John, and Harvey Molotch. 1987. *Urban Futures: The Political Economy of Place*. Berkeley: University of California Press.

Loxley, John. 2007. "The State of Community Economic Development in Winnipeg." In John Loxley, Jim Silver and Kathleen Sexsmith (eds.), *Doing Community Economic Development*. Halifax: Fernwood Publishing.

Loxley, John, with Salim Loxley. 2010. *Public Service, Private Profits: The Political Economy of Public-Private Partnerships in Canada*. Halifax and Winnipeg: Fernwood Publishing.

Mackenzie, Hugh, and Michael Rachlis. 2010. *The Sustainability of Medicare*. Ottawa: The Canadian Federation of Nurses Unions.

Mackenzie, Hugh, and Todd Scarth. 2004. *Riding Off in All Directions: An Examination of Winnipeg's New Deal*. Winnipeg: Canadian Centre for Policy Alternatives–Manitoba.

MacKinnon, Shauna. 2010. "Housing: A Major Problem in Manitoba." In Lynne Fernandez, Shauna MacKinnon and Jim Silver (eds.), *The Social Determinants of Health in Manitoba.* Winnipeg: Canadian Centre for Policy Alternatives–Manitoba.

MacKinnon, Shauna, and Sara Stevens. 2010. "Is Participation Having an Impact? Measuring Progress in Winnipeg's Inner City Through the Voices of Community-Based Program Participants." *Journal of Social Work* 10, 3.

Mann, W.E. (ed.). 1970. *Poverty and Social Policy in Canada.* Vancouver, Toronto, Montreal: Copp Clark.

Massey, Douglas S., and Nancy A. Denton. 1993. *American Apartheid: Segregation and the Making of the Underclass.* Cambridge, MA: Harvard University Press.

Meagher, Sean, and Tony Boston. 2003. "Community Engagement and the Regent Park Redevelopment." Community Engagement Team Report. Toronto.

Melles, Bruktawit. 2003. *The Relationship Between Policy, Planning and Neighbourhood Change: The Case of the Gottingen Street Neighbourhood, 1950–2000.* Master of Urban and Rural Planning, Dalhousie University.

Metropolitan Corporation of Greater Winnipeg, Planning Division. 1967. *Downtown Winnipeg.* City of Winnipeg.

Michell, Claudette, and Jake Wark. April, 2007. "Lord Selkirk Park Developments Adult Education Initiative." Honours essay, Department of Politics, University of Winnipeg.

Mikkonen, Juha, and Dennis Raphael. 2010. *Social Determinants of Health: The Canadian Facts.* Toronto: York University School of Health Policy and Management. Available at <http://www.thecanadianfacts.org/>.

Milgrom, Richard. 2003. "Sustaining Diversity: Participatory Design and the Production of Urban Space." Toronto: PhD dissertation, Graduate Programme in Environmental Studies, York University.

Mills, C. Wright. 1959. *The Sociological Imagination.* New York: Oxford University Press.

Mitchell, Katharyne. 2004. *Crossing the Neoliberal Line: Pacific Rim Migration and the Metropolis.* Philadelphia: Temple University Press.

Mochoruk, Jim, with Nancy Kardash. 2000. *The People's Co-op: The Life and Times of a North End Institution.* Halifax: Fernwood Publishing.

Morton, Suzanne. 1995. *Ideal Surroundings: Domestic Life in a Working-Class Suburb in the 1920s.* Toronto: University of Toronto Press.

Moynihan, Daniel Patrick. 1965. *The Negro Family: The Case for National Action.* Washington, DC: Office of Policy Planning and Research. Reprinted in Lee Rainwater and William Yancey (eds.), *The Moynihan Report and the Politics of Controversy.* 1967. Cambridge: MIT Press.

_____ (ed). 1969. *On Understanding Poverty.* New York: Basic Books.

Murdie, R.A. 1994. "Blacks in Near-Ghettos? Black Visible Minority Population in Metropolitan Toronto Housing Authority Public Housing Units." *Housing Studies* 9, 4.

Murray, Charles. 1984. *Losing Ground: American Social Policy: 1950–1980.* New York: Basic Books.

Musterd, Sako, and Roger Andersson. 2005. "Housing Mix, Social Mix and Social Opportunities." *Urban Affairs Review* 40, 6.

Naperstek, Arthur, Susan Freis, G. Thomas Kingsley with Dennis Dooley and Howard Lewis. 2000. *HOPE VI: Community Building Makes a Difference.* Washington, DC:

US Department of Housing and Urban Development.

National Commission on Severely Distressed Public Housing. 1992. *The Final Report of the National Commission on Severely Distressed Public Housing.* Washington, DC: Government Printing Office.

National Council of Welfare. 1998/99. *A New Poverty Line: Yes, No or Maybe?* A Discussion Paper from the National Council of Welfare. Winter. Ottawa: National Council of Welfare.

National Housing Law Project. 2002. *False HOPE: A Critical Assessment of the HOPE VI Public Housing Redevelopment Program.* Oakland, CA: National Housing Law Project.

Neckerman, Kathryn, and Joleen Kirschenman. 1991. "We'd Love to Hire Them but… The Meaning of Race for Employers." In C. Jencks and P. Peterson (eds.), *The Urban Underclass.* Washington, DC: Brookings Institute.

Nelson, Jennifer. 2008. *Razing Africville: A Geography of Racism.* Toronto: University of Toronto Press.

Newman, Katherine S. 1999. *No Shame in my Game: The Working Poor in the Inner City.* New York: Russell Sage Foundation.

Newman, Oscar. 1973. *Defensible Space.* New York: Macmillan.

NECRC (North End Community Renewal Corporation). 2008. *A Five-Year Plan for Lord Selkirk Park.* Winnipeg: NECRC.

_____. 2009. *Results of a 2009 Lord Selkirk Park Survey.* Winnipeg: NECRC.

O'Connor, Alice. 2001. *Poverty Knowledge: Social Science, Social Policy, and the Poor in Twentieth-Century U.S. History.* Princeton and Oxford: Princeton University Press.

Oakley, Deirdre, and Keri Burchfield. 2009. "Out of the Projects, Still in the Hood: The Spatial Constraints on Public-Housing Residents' Relocation in Chicago." *Journal of Urban Affairs* 31, 5.

Olsen, Byron. 1981. *A Report on the Little Mountain Housing Project.* Vancouver: Ministry of Lands, Parks and Housing.

Ornstein, Michael. 2000. *Ethno-Racial Inequality in the City of Toronto: An Analysis of the 1996 Census.* Toronto: City of Toronto.

Park, Robert E., Ernest W. Burgess and Roderick D. McKenzie. 1925. *The City.* Chicago: University of Chicago Press.

Pathways to Education. 2009. <http://www.pathwaystoeducation.ca/results.html>.

Peck, Jamie, and Adam Tickell. 2002. "Neoliberalizing Space." *Antipode* 34, 3.

_____. 2007. "Conceptualizing Neoliberalism, Thinking Thatcherism." In Helga Leitner, Jamie Peck and Eric S. Sheppard (eds.), *Contesting Neoliberalism: Urban Frontiers.* New York and London: Guildford Press.

Pomeroy, Steve. 2004. *Moving Forward: Refining the FCM Recommendations for a National Affordable Housing Strategy.* Ottawa: Federation of Canadian Municipalities.

Popkin, Susan. 2006. "The HOPE VI Program: What Has Happened to the Residents?" In Bennett, Larry, Janet L. Smith and Patricia A. Wright (eds.), *Where Are Poor People to Live? Transforming Public Housing Communities.* Armonk, NY: M.E. Sharpe.

Popkin, Susan, Bruce Katz, Mary Cunningham, Karen Brown, Jeremy Gustafson and Margery Turner. 2004. *A Decade of HOPE VI: Research Findings and Policy*

Challenges. Washington, DC: The Urban Institute.

Popkin, Susan, V.E. Gwiasda, L.M. Olson, D.P. Rosenbaum and L. Buron. 2000. *The Hidden War: Crime and the Tragedy of Public Housing in Chicago.* New Brunswick, NJ: Rutgers University Press.

Popkin, Susan, D. Levy, L. Harris, J. Comey, M. Cunningham and L. Buron. 2004. "The HOPE VI Program: What About the Residents?" *Housing Policy Debate* 15, 2.

Punter, John. 2003. *The Vancouver Achievement: Urban Planning and Design.* Vancouver: UBC Press.

Purdy, Sean. 2003a. "From Place of Hope to Outcast Space: Territorial Regulation and Tenant Resistance in Regent Park Housing Project, 1949–2001." PhD dissertation, Queen's University.

_____. 2003b. "'Ripped Off' by the System: Housing Policy, Poverty and Territorial Stigmatization in Regent Park Housing Project, 1951–1991." *Labour/Le Travail* 52.

_____. 2003c. "'It Was Tough on Everybody': Low-Income Families and Housing Hardship in Post-World War II Toronto." *Journal of Social History* 37, 2.

_____. 2005. "Framing Regent Park: The National Film Board of Canada and the Construction of 'Outcast Spaces' in the Inner City, 1953 and 1994." *Media, Culture and Society* 27, 4.

Quercia, Roberto G., and George C. Galster. 1997. "The Challenges Facing Public Housing Authorities in a Brave New World." *Housing Policy Debate* 8, 3.

Radford, Gail. 2000. "The Federal Government and Housing During the Great Depression." In John Bauman, Roger Biles and Kristin Szylvian (eds.), *From Tenements to the Taylor Homes: In Search of an Urban Housing Policy in Twentieth-Century America.* University Park, PA: Pennsylvania State University Press.

Rainwater, Lee. 1970. *Behind Ghetto Walls.* Chicago: Aldine Publishing Company.

Razack, Sharene. 2002. "When Place Becomes Race." In Sherene Razack (ed.), *Race, Space and the Law: Unmapping a White Settler Society.* Toronto: Between the Lines.

Reimer, Laura, and Associates. 2009. *Lord Selkirk Park Resource Centre Evaluation, 2009.* Winnipeg: North End Community Renewal Corporation.

Riley Park/South Cambie (RPSC). 2005. *RPSC Community Vision.*

Rose, Albert. 1958. *Regent Park.* Toronto: University of Toronto Press.

Rose, Demaris. 2004. "Discourses and Experiences of Social Mix in Gentrifying Neighbourhoods: A Montreal Case Study." *Canadian Journal of Urban Research* 13, 2.

Rosenbaum, James. 1995. "Housing Mobility Strategies for Changing the Geography of Opportunity." *Housing Policy Debate* 6, 1.

Rosenbaum, James, Lisa Reynolds and Stefanie Deluca. 2002. "How Do Places Matter? The Geography of Opportunity, Self-Efficacy and a Look Inside the Black Box of Residential Mobility." *Housing Studies* 17, 1.

RPNI (Regent Park Neighbourhood Initiative). 2006. *Embracing a Changing Landscape: A Community Effort in Planning for a New Regent Park.* <www.toronto.ca/revitalization/regent_park/pdf/commity_plan_sept2007_appendix2.pdf>.

Rosenbaum, James, Linda Stroh and Cathy A. Flynn. 1998. "Lake Parc Place: A Study of Mixed-Income Housing." *Housing Policy Debate* 9, 4.

Rushowy, Kristin. 2007. "A Million Dollar Model." *Toronto Star* April 20.

Sahak, Jaihun. 2008. "Race, Space and Place: Exploring Toronto's Regent Park from a Marxist Perspective." M.A. Thesis, Toronto: Ryerson University.

Sandercock, Leonie. 2006. "An Anatomy of Civic Ambition in Vancouver: Toward Humane Density." In William S. Saunders (ed.), *Urban Planning Today.* Minneapolis: University of Minnesota Press.

Sarkissian, Wendy. 1976. "The Idea of Social Mix in Town Planning: An Historical Review." *Urban Studies* 13.

Sarlo, Christopher. 1996. *Poverty in Canada.* Second Edition. Vancouver: Fraser Institute.

Schill, Michael H., Samantha Friedman and Emily Rosenbaum. 1998. "The Housing Conditions of Immigrants in New York City." *Journal of Housing Research* 9, 2.

Schippling, Richard. 2007. "Public Housing Redevelopment: Residents' Experiences with Relocation from Phase I of Toronto's Regent Park Revitalization." Waterloo, ON: M.A. Thesis, Planning, University of Waterloo.

Seshia, Maya. 2010. "Naming Systemic Violence in Winnipeg's Street Sex Trade." *Canadian Journal of Urban Research* 19, 1 (Summer).

Sewell, John. 1993. *The Shape of the City: Toronto Struggles with Modern Planning.* Toronto: University of Toronto Press.

_____. 1994. *Houses and Homes: Housing for Canadians.* Toronto: James Lorimer.

Silver, Jim. 2002. *Building on our Strengths: Inner-City Priorities for a Renewed Tri-Level Development Agreement.* Winnipeg: Canadian Centre for Policy Alternatives–Manitoba.

_____. 2006a. *In Their Own Voices: Building Urban Aboriginal Communities.* Halifax: Fernwood Publishing.

_____. 2006b. *North End Winnipeg's Lord Selkirk Park Housing Developments: History, Comparative Context, Prospects.* Winnipeg: Canadian Centre for Policy Alternatives–Manitoba.

_____. 2006c. *Gentrification in West Broadway: Contested Space in a Winnipeg Inner City Neighbourhood.* Winnipeg: Canadian Centre for Policy Alternatives–Manitoba.

_____. 2007a. *Unearthing Resistance: Aboriginal Women in the Lord Selkirk Park Housing Developments.* Winnipeg: Canadian Centre for Policy Alternatives–Manitoba.

_____. 2007b. "Persistent Poverty and the Promise of Community Solutions." In Les Samuelson and Wayne Antony (eds.), *Power and Resistance: Critical Thinking About Canadian Social Issues.* Halifax: Fernwood Publishing.

_____. 2008. *Public Housing Risks and Alternatives: Uniacke Square in North End Halifax.* Halifax and Winnipeg: Canadian Centre for Policy Alternatives–Nova Scotia/Manitoba.

_____. 2009a. "Unearthing Resistance: Aboriginal Women in the Lord Selkirk Park Housing Developments." In Liliane Rodriguez (ed.), *Aboriginal Governance and Globalization: Proceedings of the International Symposium held at the University of Winnipeg, January 31–February 2, 2008.* Winnipeg: University of Winnipeg.

_____. 2009b. "Complex Poverty and Home-Grown Solutions in Two Prairie Cities." In Sharon McKay, Don Fuchs and Ivan Brown (eds.), *Passion for Action in Child and Family Services: Voices from the Prairie Region.* Regina: Canadian Plains Research Center.

_____. 2010a. "Spatially Concentrated Racialized Poverty as a Social Determinant of Health: The Case of Winnipeg's Inner City." In Lynne Fernandez, Shauna

MacKinnon and Jim Silver (eds.), *The Social Determinants of Health in Manitoba*. Winnipeg: Canadian Centre for Policy Alternatives–Manitoba.

_____. 2010b. "Segregated City: 100 Years of Poverty in Winnipeg." In Paul Thomas and Curtis Brown (eds.), *Government and Politics in Manitoba*. Winnipeg: University of Manitoba Press.

Silver, Jim, and John Loxley. 2007. "An Introduction to Community Economic Development." In John Loxley, Jim Silver and Kathleen Sexsmith (eds.), *Doing Community Economic Development*. Halifax: Fernwood Publishing.

Silver, Jim, and Owen Toews. 2009. "Combating Poverty in Winnipeg's Inner City, 1960s–1990s: Thirty Years of Hard-Earned Lessons." *Canadian Journal of Urban Research* 18, 1 (Summer).

Slater, Tom. 2004. "Municipally Managed Gentrification in South Parkdale." *The Canadian Geographer* 48, 3.

_____. 2005. "Gentrification in Canada's Cities: From Social Mix to Social Tectonics." In R. Atkinson and G. Bridge (eds.), *Gentrification in a Global Context: The New Urban Colonialism*. NY, Routledge.

Smith, Doug. 1990. *Joe Zuken: Citizen and Activist*. Toronto: Lorimer.

Smith, Janet L. 2002. "HOPE VI and the New Urbanism: Eliminating Low-Income Housing to Make Mixed-Income Communities." *Planners Network* 15, 1.

_____. 2006. "The Chicago Housing Authority's Plan for Transformation." In Bennett, Larry, Janet L. Smith and Patricia A. Wright (eds.), *Where Are Poor People to Live? Transforming Public Housing Communities*. Armonk, NY: M.E. Sharpe.

Smith, Neil. 1996. *The New Urban Frontier: Gentrification and the Revanchist City*. London and New York: Routledge.

_____. 2002. "New Globalization; New Urbanism: Gentrification as Global Urban Strategy." *Antipode* 34, 3.

Social Planning and Research Council of BC. 2008. *Still on Our Streets: Results of the 2008 Metro Vancouver Homeless Count*. Vancouver: Metro Vancouver Regional Steering Committee on Homelessness.

Stanford, Jim. 2008. "Toronto Fiscal Panel: The View From Inside." *The Progressive Economics Forum*. <http://www.progressive-economics.ca/2008/03/02/toronto-fiscal-panel-the-view-from-inside/>.

Statistics Canada. 2001. *Census of Canada*.

_____. 2006. *Census of Canada*.

Stephenson, Gordon. 1957. *A Redevelopment Study of Halifax, Nova Scotia*. Halifax: The Corporation of the City of Halifax.

Swanson, Jean. 2001. *Poor-Bashing: The Politics of Exclusion*. Toronto: Between the Lines.

Teeple, Gary. 2000. *Globalization and the Decline of Social Reform: Into the Twenty-First Century*. Expanded second edition. Toronto: Garamond.

Toronto Community Housing Corporation (TCHC). September 2007a. *Regent Park Social Development Plan. Executive Summary*.

_____. September 2007b. *Regent Park Social Development Plan. Part I: Context*.

_____. September 2007c. *Regent Park Social Development Plan. Part II: Best Practices for Social Inclusion in Mixed-Income Communities*.

_____. September 2007d. *Regent Park Social Development Plan. Part III: Strategies for Social Inclusion*.

Turbov, Mindy, and Valerie Piper. 2005. *HOPE VI and Mixed-Finance Redevelopments: A Catalyst for Neighbourhood Renewal.* Washington, DC: Brookings Institute.

United Way of Greater Toronto. 2004. *Poverty by Postal Code: The Geography of Neighbourhood Poverty 1981–2001.* Toronto: United Way of Greater Toronto and Canadian Council on Social Development.

Urban Social Development Project. 1970. "Social and Mental Health Survey, Montreal, 1966 Summary Report." In W.E. Mann (ed.), *Poverty and Social Policy in Canada.* Vancouver, Toronto, Montreal: Copp Clark.

Usiskin, Roz. N.D. "Selkirk Ave Revisited: The Hub of Winnipeg's North End, the Jewish Experience 1905-–1950. Winnipeg: unpublished paper.

Vale, Lawrence. 2002. *Reclaiming Public Housing: A Half Century of Struggle in Three Public Neighbourhoods.* Cambridge, MA: Harvard University Press.

van Berkel, Lis. 2005. "Window Pains." *The Coast* May 26–June 2.

_____. 2007. "Where Goes the Neighbourhood?" *The Coast* April 12.

van Kempen, Ronald, K. Dekker, S. Hall and I Tosics (eds.). 2005. *Restructuring Large Housing Estates in Europe.* Bristol: Policy Press.

Vancouver. 2007. "Administrative Report to the Standing Committee on Planning and Environment." July 26. From the Director of Planning in Consultation with the Director of the Housing Centre.

Venkatesh, Sudhir Alladi. 2000. *American Project: The Rise and Fall of a Modern Ghetto.* Cambridge, MA and London: Harvard University Press.

_____. 2006. *Off the Books: The Underground Economy of the Urban Poor.* Cambridge, MA, and London: Harvard University Press.

von Hoffman, Alexander. 1996. "High Ambitions: The Past and Future of American Low-Income Housing Policy." *Housing Policy Debate* 7, 3.

_____. 2000. "Why They Built Pruitt-Igoe." In John Bauman, Roger Biles and Kristin Szylvian (eds.), *From Tenements to the Taylor Homes: In Search of an Urban Housing Policy in Twentieth-Century America.* University Park, PA: Pennsylvania State University Press.

Wacquant, Loic. 2008. *Urban Outcasts: A Comparative Sociology of Advanced Marginality.* Cambridge, UK: Polity Press.

Wade, Jill. 1994. *Houses for All: The Struggle for Social Housing in Vancouver, 1919–50.* Vancouver: UBC Press.

Wanzel, Grant. 2006. "Panel on Rebuilding Place: Creating Viable Communites." April 19. CHRA Congress.

Watt, Paul. 2008. "Underclass and 'Ordinary People' Discourses: Representing/Re-presenting Council Tenants in a Housing Campaign." *Critical Discourse Studies* 5, 4.

Whitzman, Carolyn. 2009. *Suburb, Slum, Urban Village: Transformations in Toronto's Parkdale Neighbourhood, 1875–2002.* Vancouver: UBC Press.

Williams, Rhonda. 2004. *The Politics of Public Housing: Black Women's Struggles Against Urban Inequality.* Oxford: Oxford University Press.

Wilson, William Julius, 1978. *The Declining Significance of Race: Blacks and Changing American Institutions.* Chicago: University of Chicago Press.

_____. 1987. *The Truly Disadvantaged: The Inner City, the Underclass, and Public Policy.* Chicago and London: University of Chicago Press.

_____. 1996. *When Work Disappears: The World of the New Urban Poor.* New York: Alfred

A. Knopf.

Winks, Robin W. 1997. *The Blacks in Canada*. Montreal and Kingston: McGill-Queen's University Press.

Wright, Patricia A. 2006. "Community Resistance to CHA Transformation: The History, Evolution, Struggles and Accomplishments of the Coalition to Protect Public Housing." In Larry Bennett, Janet L. Smith and Patricia A. Wright (eds.), *Where Are Poor People to Live? Transforming Public Housing Communities*. Armonk, NY: M.E. Sharpe.

Yalnizyan, Armine. 1998. *The Growing Gap: A Report on Growing Inequality Between Rich and Poor in Canada*. Toronto: Centre for Social Justice.

Yauk, Thomas B. 1973. "Residential and Business Relocation From Urban Renewal Areas: A Case Study — The Lord Selkirk Park Experience." Master of City Planning thesis, University of Manitoba.

About the Author

Jim Silver is professor and Director of the Urban and Inner-City Studies program at the University of Winnipeg. He is a founding member and current board member of the Canadian Centre for Policy Alternatives-Manitoba and has written extensively about inner-city and poverty-related issues, especially in Winnipeg. Among several books, he is most recently the co-editor of *The Social Determinants of Health in Manitoba* and *Doing Community Economic Development*, and author of *In Their Own Voices: Building Urban Aboriginal Communities*.

More new titles from Fernwood Publishing...

Activism that Works

*Elizabeth Whitmore, Maureen G.
Wilson & Avery Calhoun, eds.*

pb 9781552664117 $19.95 160pp Rights: World March 2011

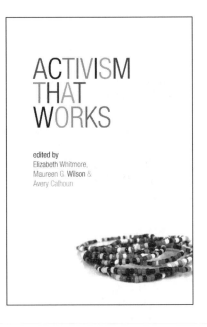

How can we understand "success" in relation to social justice and environmental
activism? How do activists themselves
determine or define their effectiveness?
Activism That Works shares the stories of
eight diverse social justice movements,
from Oxfam Canada, to the Calgary Raging
Grannies, to the Youth Project of Halifax,
as they contemplate their own successes.
What we discover is that success is not
measured only in large-scale social reform
but is also found in moments of connection — in building relationships and raising
awareness. Taking the lead from these stories, the authors contextualize and analyze
success within social justice activism in Canada. Understanding their work as a contribution to the movements challenging the domination of free market ideology,
the authors hope this book will offer a space for reflecting on the contributions and
impacts of activist groups — and provide meaningful insights into what success
means in the struggle against neoliberal capitalism.

ELIZABETH (BESSA) WHITMORE is professor emerita at Carleton University's School
of Social Work. MAUREEN G. WILSON is a professor in the Faculty of Social Work and
co-chair of the Consortium for Peace Studies at the University of Calgary. AVERY
CALHOUN is an associate professor of social work at the University of Calgary.

www.fernwoodpublishing.ca

Broke but Unbroken

Grassroots Social Movements
and Their Radical Solutions
to Poverty

Augusta Dwyer

pb 9781552664063 $19.95 144pp Rights: Canada May 2011

In *Broke but Unbroken*, journalist Augusta
Dwyer takes us on an inspiring journey
through the slums and villages of Brazil,
Indonesia, India and Argentina as she
meets with organizers from some of the
most successful grassroots social movements struggling against poverty. These
organizers are not representatives from
NGOs or aid organizations based in developed nations but the poor themselves —
people who know intimately the reality of
struggling for land, food, housing and the
right to control their own resources and means of production. It is these movements, built from the ground up by the very people affected by poverty, that have
achieved the most successes in ameliorating the conditions of the poor and providing real solutions to global poverty.

As we travel with Dwyer through rural and urban landscapes, too often devas-
tated by the demands of development, we meet people who have risked their
homes, families and even their lives to affect real change in the world. The stories
they share so openly and warmly are not merely accounts of economic or political
success but are stories of empowerment and hope that dramatically portray the
potency of collective action.

In the beautiful prose of an accomplished writer, this book introduces us to extraordinary grassroots movements — and encourages us to learn the lessons they offer
about successfully challenging power and changing the world.

AUGUSTA DWYER is an award-winning independent journalist and the author of
Into the Amazon: Chico Mendes and the Struggle for the Rainforest and *On the Line: Life
on the U.S.-Mexico Border.*

www.fernwoodpublishing.ca

Doing Anti-Oppressive Practice
Social Justice Social Work,
2nd Edition

Donna Baines, ed.

pb 9781552664100 pb $34.95
hb 9781552664285 hb $59.95
360pp Rights: World March 2011

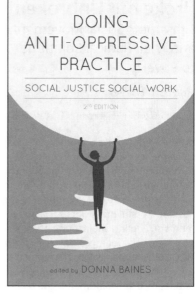

Doing Anti-Oppressive Practice introduces students to the emerging tradition, the historical and theoretical roots and the specific contexts of anti-oppressive social work practice. AOP understands the problems faced by clients as rooted in the socio-political structure of society rather than in the personal characteristics of the clients themselves, and argues that social change must be a key component of social work practice. Using practice vignettes, personal experience and case work examples to discuss a variety of issues, this updated edition adds a new chapter on the theoretical basis of AOP as well as several practice chapters dealing with issues of child protection, poverty and welfare rights, disability rights, working with unions and standardized assessment procedures.

Praise for the first edition
"This has been a helpful text for examining issues of gender and oppression through an intersectional lens. The book not only introduces 'anti-oppressive practice' as a current form of progressive social work, but also provides helpful illustrations on topics such as indigenous pathways to anti-oppressive practice, bridging the practice-activism divide, anti-oppressive practice in child welfare, and restructuring and everyday resistance. A range of Canadian authors describe strategies, highlight issues and raise practical dilemmas inherent in practicing social work from an anti-oppressive perspective."

— *Lyn Ferguson, Faculty of Social Work, University of Manitoba*

DONNA BAINES is an associate professor of labour studies and social work at McMaster University.

www.fernwoodpublishing.ca